HOPE AND A FUTURE

A Story of Resiliency

A Memoir

By

Karima S. Hyman, MA

WGWPublishing.com

ISBN: 978-1-7324781-6-9

Editing: Wandah Gibbs, Ed. D.

Printed in the USA

WGW Publishing Inc.,

Rochester, NY

About the Cover...

To find answers to most of life's quandaries, look no further than nature. Wallace D. Wattles states in his book, *The Science of Getting Rich,* that there is always an analogy in nature. See the mountains and valleys. That is life; if you are in a valley, keep going you will soon make it to the mountain top. That probably won't last long either, however, and you will soon descend into a valley. Such is life. Also, you see the trees. A mentor once taught me that as far as the tree's roots go into the ground, that is the same measure that the tree's branches reach out towards the sky. Your hardships are in direct proportion to your successes. Also, you will see water. Everything is always moving; you are either moving forwards or backwards. Finally, in the same way that the water meets and recedes from the shore, there is an ebb and flow to life.

This Book Is Dedicated to My Dad,

For teaching me that I could have, do, or become anything I wanted to. You loved me. You told me that you wanted me to write a book and that you wanted me "to make a million dollars." You believed in me. I will forever be grateful that you were my dad. I will continue to make it my life's purpose to transfer the love you gave to me, to do my part to make this world a better place, and to make you proud. I know you are in paradise proudly looking down on all of your offspring. I love you, dad.

Clifford N. Hyman, Sr.
October 25, 1931 - September 29, 2020

Introduction

This is a book about resiliency. Its purpose is to relay the message that we all have a story. We all started from somewhere. Some people's starting points are more challenging than others. But no matter how insurmountable the mountains and valleys may seem, you can and will make it through. The pressures of life are not meant to break you nor destroy you. The pressures of life are to make you stronger so that you can tell your story in the end that it may serve to help thousands if not millions of others going through similar situations. Nothing happens by accident. Everything happens for a purpose and that purpose is for you to learn, grow, and serve.

Table of Contents

Chapter 1

In the Beginning

I was born at Albert Einstein Hospital in the Olney section of Philadelphia. At that time my mom, older sister, older brother, and I lived in Cornwell's Heights, a section in Northeast Philadelphia. When I was two, we moved to one of my grandparent's properties on Harold Street in North Philadelphia (North Philly for short). We were part of the Weston family that occupied many of the homes on that block. There was also a "Hyman" cousin around the corner. I was surrounded by family.

I have fond memories of my childhood back then. My older sister was like a second mother to me. She's 10 years older than me and my brother is four years older than me. My sister and I had the back room and my brother had the middle room. The memories I have of my siblings are scarce in that home during that time. I realized much later that it's because they weren't there during the week, except during the summer months.

My sister was my world back then. I loved her so much. I recall listening to *I Wanna be Your Lover* by Prince and Michael Jackson's *Off the Wall* album on her record player in the back room. I also remember her teaching me to sing to *Silly* by Denise Williams. "No,

Karima," she would say, "your voice is supposed to sound like hers." I was introduced to The Sylvers, Stephanie Mills, Switch...and so many other musical artists early on. My brother constantly snuck into our room at night because he was, as Charlotte (my sister) would say, "scaaared of the dark!" Chris wouldn't laugh but we thought that was just sooo funny. Charlotte often teased Chris back then.

Charlotte and Chris have a different biological father than I do. They are both light-skinned. This is a significant detail in the African-American culture. And although I was not even aware of the difference, I was made to become aware of this difference a little later in life. I will discuss this briefly later in this book. However, it is true that in many colonized nations throughout the world, where indigenous people are of a darker hue, a system of colorism exists and has been perpetuated throughout generations in many cultures. My experience, however, is the African-American one, and though I never had a problem with my skin color, it became clear later on in my life that perhaps being brown or dark-skinned was something of which I should be ashamed. But honestly, those underlying insecurities engrained in society have never really affected me. I don't have a problem with my skin tone. I think it's becoming.

I remember going to daycare at the Cecil B. Moore Recreation Center on 22nd Street, also known as "The Center" for daycare. Mrs. McCoy was my preschool teacher, as was true for many of the kids who grew up in that neighborhood. We performed in fashion shows and talent shows there. I thought I was going to be a star and I loved being on stage. I knew I was special.

I also remember attending school in Center City close to my parents' jobs. I went to an Islamic school below Broad & Spring Garden Streets. My mom worked across the street at the County Assistance Office. I was always so proud that my mom worked for the state for over 30 years. My dad worked in that same area in sales. Before I was born, he worked closely with Malcolm X on his public relations team. While I attended the Islamic school, he sold commercial cleaning products. During that time, my dad was interviewed pretty regularly for his views and opinions on the Muslim movement and his work with Malcolm X. I remember my mom saying on several occasions, "Karima, your dad is on T.V.!"

One day some kids and I were playing in front of the school during recess. I remember that a lady I didn't recognize approached me, "Hi Karima," she said in a pleasant voice. She had a scarf on her head. "Do you like dolls?" she asked. I nodded, "yes." She continued, "come on, we can go to my house and play with some dolls." I began to walk with her down an alley, but then I heard my teacher call my name, "Karima, it's time to go in…" I ran towards him and went inside with the rest of my class. I turned my head to see the lady disappearing into the alley. To this day, I don't know who she was. I told my mother about that event when I got older and she said it was probably one of my dad's girlfriends. Thinking about it now kind of sends chills up my spine. What were her plans had I followed her?

That school doubled up as a Masjid, a place where Muslims go to worship. I remember feeling sad downstairs in the Masjid because I had to be separated from my dad. I don't remember worshiping or praying but I do remember that upon entering he had to go on one side of the building whereas I was handed off to a woman who took me by the hand and walked me to the other side to be with the ladies. When my dad picked me up after worship or school, we sometimes went to a trolley-themed restaurant next door.

At home, I followed my dad around from room to room and did whatever he did. On Sundays, he read the paper and gave me the "funnies," then I would read them while he read his section. I remember feeling sad whenever a football game came on. I didn't know what to do with myself because any other time, I was always up under my dad. But when football was on, he literally paid no attention to me. For so long, when a football game would be on, and I heard the referee whistle, a feeling of sadness would come over me. It was a fleeting feeling of sadness. That's a level of post-traumatic stress disorder (PTSD). It's not a diagnosis of PTSD but it is one criteria: marked physiological reactions to internal or external cues that symbolize or resemble an aspect of the traumatic event(s) (DSM-5). It's minimal, I know. It's just interesting how we all have some level of trauma.

My dad was very strict about the foods he'd allow me to eat. I couldn't eat any junk food. I couldn't eat pork or anything with pork or lard in it (*Jello-O*, marshmallows, etc.). He used to eat dinner for breakfast. I read in my cultural diversity class, that many cultures do this as it provides you with a lot of protein and you'll only have to eat one big meal a day. To this day, with the exception of coffee and a small pastry of some kind, I often skip breakfast as I cannot wait to get to dinner. Another thing My dad used to do; he'd cut up peaches and cover them in milk and brown sugar in a bowl. Everything was brown; brown sugar, molasses, wheat bread, brown eggs, wheat pancakes, wheat germ, and wheat flour for the bran muffins he taught my mother to make. I used to get so angry at the foods he made us eat because I didn't know anyone else who ate like that. Years later, it turns out he was way ahead of his time in so many ways.

My dad was my strength. He loved me so much and I felt that. In preparation for a ceremony during a family reunion, I had to interview him. When I asked, "dad, what was the happiest moment in your life?" He answered, "the happiest moment in my life was when I had my daughter, Karima."

My dad lived in and out of the house. I believe he really did try to live in the same home with his child(ren) and remain a part of a nuclear family. When I was around three, I remember living with him for a while in the Northeast section of Philadelphia. I went to

5

school up there. He used to do my hair and I remember feeling so embarrassed. He would also take me over to my cousins and have them do my hair. My dad told me later that there had been a fire at the apartment where he lived so I guess that's how I ended up back with my mother.

When I was around three or four years old, I remember being at a lady's house with her and her four kids. We all seemed to get along really well and one day as we were playing, there was a commotion at the door. The lady of the house told us to go into the basement to play so us kids all went downstairs. Suddenly, I looked up through the basement window and caught a glimpse of my mom and her best friend. My mom was crying so I started crying too. Apparently, my dad had kidnapped me and brought me to his other family's house which was an hour and a half away from where I lived. My mom had come to get me back. Because no one had official, legal custody of me, she was turned away, to leave without me. My soon-to-be stepmom was too afraid to hand me over to my mom. She later apologized to me for that for the longest. We had become extremely close in later years. I believe my dad really wanted to be ever-present in my life and he really did try. He had the right intentions though he went about it the wrong way.

Soon after that incident, my mom had come to reclaim me, I was sitting in the circle at preschool when my teacher walked into the classroom accompanied by a woman (whom I couldn't see clearly at first). "Karima, who is this?" said my teacher. I ran towards her and screamed "mommy!" My mom then scooped me up and ran down the hall, attempting to hide me under her coat. I remember the teacher saying, "wait! She needs her jacket!" and my mom shouting as she ran out of the building: "she has one in the car!" When we got outside, my brother Chris was there waiting in the car.

My mother's nickname for me was "Remy." I'm told I was a little smart aleck when I was young probably because I was the youngest of my siblings and cousins. My mom used to smoke *Salem Lights* and drink a lot of *Pepsi*. Once we were upstairs in her room while she was on the phone and I asked her to make me some pancakes. She replied, "Karima, we don't have any pancakes." My response was, "I bet you got some *Pepsi* and cigarettes though!" She told me this sometime later and I remember having said it. There were many other times I recall having a smart mouth. Throughout the years however, my bravado and confidence dwindled.

Early on; along with extended family and friends, we went on skiing trips, trips to Cape Cod, and camping trips. Today, we laugh remembering how my dad crashed into the lobby of the skiing lodge, calling to my mother saying, "Emma...Emma, look at me!" – CRASH! And another time when we went to get fresh spring water, my dad stepped on a beehive. Bees started chasing us, stinging my cousin and my brother.

Meanwhile, my dad tucked me safely under his coat as we ran.

There were other good times too, when my dad took my cousins, some of the neighborhood kids, and my brother and I to a swimming hole in *Wissahickon Valley*, a section of Fairmont Park. There, we dove off a cliff into *Wissahickon Creek*, hoping to jump into the exact spot that's 15 feet deep. Although many people still do this today, it is now illegal. I recall my dad hosting skating parties at *United Skates of America.* I also recall going to see the movie, *E.T. the Extra-Terrestrial.* That was the first and only time I ever saw my father cry. My dad also took me to football games to see the Eagles play. I remember freezing and I remember feeling the same chill each time he took us to the *Thanksgiving* and *Mummer's Day* Parades.

Though we had good times, I don't recall feeling much stability during my early years. I spent a lot of time with my dad's sister, my Aunt Vivian. One day, my mom came to pick me up and I started crying because I wanted to stay. She said, "awww...Karima, you're hurting my feelings." I don't remember if she let me stay longer with Aunt Vivian or if she took me with her. That really must have hurt her as a mother. I'm not sure exactly why I had that reaction. I do however remember feeling loved by my mother when I was little and being her "baby."

Early on, I remember my parents having somewhat of a tumultuous relationship. I remember hearing a lot of arguments between my parents. I remember sitting at the top of the steps with my older brother and sister and my sister saying, "Karima, go down there and break it up; he's your father". I didn't go. I, then, remember hearing him storm out of the house.

At some point, my mom didn't have me enrolled in school. I would just go across the street to Mrs. White's house and sit there all day. My dad later expressed to me his displeasure about this. However, I am not sure if this is when he took me up to the Northeast to live with him or if it was when he took me to live in Lancaster, PA and enrolled me in school there.

During my childhood on Harold Street however, I have a lot of good memories, especially whenever my siblings were also at home. We were surrounded by multiple generations of family and close friends of the family. For many years, prior to us moving there, my grandmother owned a beauty shop at the top of the block called "Weston's Beautyrama". During the summer, the older kids in my sister's age group lit fire crackers and turned on the water-plug AKA fire hydrant, and "dunked" or "baptized" those who couldn't run away fast enough. We sometimes stayed out until the early morning hours playing games on the steps. We played *Red Light/Green Light (apple, peaches, pumpkin pie...who's not ready holler, "I"!* – was our version of *marco/polo).* We played *Hide and Seek, Mother May I,* and *Dumb School* which consisted of the "teacher" asking a question and with each correct answer, you got to move up one step.

When I was six, I joined Charlotte and Chris at our maternal grandparent's home in McKinley, a section of Elkins Park, PA (Abington Township). With my grandparents having legal guardianship, we lived there so we could attend school in that district. Because my mom had gone to school in North Philly, she had been really behind when she came up to Abington for high school. She decided that that her kids would never go to an inner-city school. I was traumatized however because I'd been plucked away from my parents and shipped to these strangers in this unfamiliar environment. I didn't really know my grandparents back then.

It must have been a day that I didn't have school or school hadn't started for me yet, but I remember my sister just leaving me in this house with "these people." I was not harmed, just lonely during the day. I felt a void just like at Mrs. White's house. I remember thinking, "someone else that I love is leaving me". Though they were my grandparents, to me they were just strangers. I cried my eyes out then sat at the piano and started angrily hitting the keys with a pestle (a tool used for crushing pills). My grandparents had a decorative wood mortar and pestle grinding machine on top of the piano. I feel bad when I think back on it because that wasn't like me to do something like that. I was simply a traumatized child, crying out. When my grandfather found out he told me to hold out my hands then proceeded to hit my hands with his belt. With that one minor exception, however, I remember my pop-pop being a very sweet and tender man: a remarkable provider and family man. He built that home in Elkins Park from the ground up in the early sixties, owned many properties throughout the city and worked multiple jobs to provide for his family. He adored my grandmother, his "Libby." I often say, "they don't make 'em like that anymore".

I started first grade at McKinley Elementary School when I was six years old. My brother, who was in the fourth grade, and I walked to school together. We had to leave for school at 8:20 am to be to school by 8:40 am. I would be with my brother or the other neighborhood kids and we'd meet up on a corner or would just call out to each other as we walked down the street. Back then, we were all friends and I don't recall much division. We had to walk through the neighborhood, across the baseball field, down the path, and through the woods every day. It's a wonder that during my six years of attending McKinley, I never heard of anything unnerving happening to anyone on the walking path. I'm sure however, that when "the walkers" (as we were called) came upon the wooded section, I was not the only kid who felt a little apprehension. I felt this way everyday,. I also remember feeling a tinge of relief whenever I made it to the other side, when seeing that brown school building. Every day, I remember hearing a silent, still, small voice, saying, "you made it."

My older sister taught me everything from how to do my hair to how to bathe. I remember one night when I was bored, I put a whole bunch of petroleum jelly in my hair and she yelled at me, "why did you do that?! Now you're going to have a whole bunch of lint in your hair!" She was right. Sure enough, the next day I woke up and had a whole bunch of lint in my hair. I was curious by nature so I was always getting into something. I've always been inquisitive and a wonderer which can be both good and bad I suppose. I am the type that will try almost anything once.

We were really blessed to live in that community at that time. Often, after school we'd go to Alverthorpe Park, which was just around the corner from my grandparent's house. There, we played miniature golf, tennis, badminton, basketball, and rode our bikes on the trails...all for free. To use any of their equipment we simply had to trade in something for collateral in exchange for borrowing a tennis racquet, basketball, or other equipment. Those were simpler times.

At the end of my second-grade year, my sister went to live with her paternal grand-parents and then away to college. I was eight at the time and barely saw her between 1983-1985. But then in 1983 my cousins from Ohio came to live with us. I remember thinking of them as the tall and cool cousins. My oldest female cousin, whom I thought was the coolest girl on the planet, teased me mercilessly. She is light-skinned whereas I am brown-skinned. She used to call me all kinds of derogatory terms pertaining to my complexion.

I came to accept this kind of treatment from her and other members on my mom's side of the family; as far as being made to feel like an outsider. Nonetheless, when my cousins came to live with us for those two years, my quality of life improved. After my sister left for college, many of the basic life necessities had left with her. When my cousins arrived, we suddenly had plenty of food and cable TV. I just idolized my older cousin and I remember following her from room to room. She would yell, "stop following me." Her mother, my aunt, would say, "she loves you!"

My grandparent's house was dark and unstimulating. My aunt helped me get dressed in the mornings because it was so cold in that house in the winter. She also kneeled by the side of my bed with me at night and taught me *The Lord's Prayer*. My grandfather passed away when I was in the fourth grade and soon after, my aunt left and my cousins followed. Then it was just my brother and I again.

During my fourth-grade year, I remember going to school with holes in my jeans (not stylish at the time), un-bathed, and malnourished. I was terribly neglected. I almost failed that grade. It seems that my mom had checked out of her responsibilities. In her defense, she had lost her father and my dad had fathered a son with and re-married my step-mother around that same time.

The summers in North Philly on Harold Street, were perfect, however. We continued to run up and down the street and stay out, talking and playing often until sunrise. Additionally, my parents enrolled my brother and I in summer camps. We began taking piano lessons though neither my brother nor I enjoyed it. We took turns coming to pick each other up from piano, telling the teacher that we had something we needed to do; just so we could get out of taking piano lessons. Then, we then had to hide out in the neighborhood for an hour to pass the time away.

I also went to *Vacation Bible School* (VBS) with all of the other neighborhood kids. It was crazy because a van would stop by and pick-up anybody who wanted to go and they'd take us to Berean Baptist Church for about an hour a day for a week in July. Half the time, I don't even think our parents knew where we were. It was just that kind of environment back then. Many times, we just walked into each other's houses and sat on the couch and watched TV, even if the person who lived there didn't seem to be home. I remember one day I was taking a nap (as I was accustomed to doing) and a neighbor came in and sat in my mom's room waiting for me to get up. When I awoke, she asked, "are you going to Bible school?" I thought, "oh okay," nodded my head "yes" and out the door we went. Our parents were nowhere to be found. The environment was just that trusting, family oriented, and warm. We attended Vacation Bible School and always came home without incident.

When my dad still lived with us, while all the other kids and I would be playing outside, he'd yell out the window, "Karima! – come in and take a nap!" I was always so embarrassed. This went on until the summer of 1984. I thought I was too old to take naps, plus none of the other kids had to, but my dad was extremely strict and serious about molding his kids properly, when he was around. He believed that naps helped me grow. As previously noted, we were only allowed to eat certain foods; I had to wear orthopedic shoes to prevent back problems, and to protect the arches in my feet. We didn't celebrate holidays or go to the movies. We had to drink water with every meal. We weren't allowed to get out of bed until my dad got up.

I eventually associated this limited lifestyle with being a Muslim. As a kid, I thought, "why would anybody want to be a Muslim? You don't get to do anything that makes you happy." I now know that was a very skewed way to practice religion. In fact, it really had nothing to do with the practice of Islam from what I now understand. By the time my parents got divorced, I was actually happy. I knew that they loved each other, but even as a child, I could tell they were incompatible. I loved my dad but I couldn't live with his (what I thought at the time) irrational and strict ways.

My dad was a proud man who took pleasure in raising his children well. I felt really proud around him and always wanted him to come to my school when possible because he looked so debonair. He always wore nice suits, cologne, and carried a brief case. Also, I loved going for a drive with him in his Oldsmobile while we listened to John Coltrane. I didn't appreciate it then but now I love listening to Coltrane and that style of jazz. It reminds me of his car and the smell of his cologne. His vehicle was always clean (we weren't allowed to eat in the car), and I always felt so important and safe when I was around him. He even took me on daddy-daughter dates and opened the car door for me to get in. In terms of material possessions, my dad didn't really buy me much but morally, emotionally, and mentally he didn't take anything away. In fact, he encouraged every little thing I wanted to do and try. That taught me that if you can't do anything for your children just don't take any of their internal resources away from them and always encourage their internal power. This also taught me that if someone truly loves you, they will love you whether you buy them material possessions or not.

My parents say they were married and people have told me that they were, but I've never seen any paperwork. I do believe they were married however, because one time when I was sleeping in my mom's bed, which I did until I was about 11 years old (family lived with us and took my room), I overheard her on the phone with her boyfriend. She thought I was asleep but

I heard her say, "my divorce finally went through." Every shut eye is not sleep. I've been told that my dad did indeed marry my mom, primarily because he didn't want me to feel illegitimate. I do have many pictures of them together. They are genuine friends.

Growing up, my siblings and I really did have the best of both worlds. We had the suburban academic and social exposure and the close community experience of urban life, with family living close by. Back in the 70's and 80's our block was the perfect place to be raised. It was family-oriented and safe. Everybody came over to our block to play. I even remember, as the water-plug was on at the top of the block, a now very famous celebrity and I were at the corner of 23rd and Harold talking briefly while dipping our feet in the water as it flowed down the street. In spite of my family dysfunction, for the most part, I thought my childhood was pretty ideal. Whenever I see the movie *Crooklyn* by Spike Lee, I see many similarities to my childhood.

During the summers, I went to camp and my cousins from North Philly and my family would go to Virginia Beach or Maryland for a weekend. We went "crabbing" and to the amusement parks. One year we went to Kings Dominion and another year we went to Busch Gardens. It wasn't perfect, but from what I could remember, much of my childhood was happy. Also, when we went crabbing, we'd only catch four or five crabs altogether, but when we got home, my Uncle Chip (who lived directly across the street from us), would magically have bushels of crabs ready and seasoned to perfection. I figured he must've caught them because we sure hadn't. Later, I learned he'd stopped off before we got home to purchase bushels of crabs. While reflecting on this I am filled with nostalgia. For me, life in the summer was absolutely perfect!

When I wasn't at summer camp, I would wake up and watch *Gidget*, *Fantasy Island*, *Gilligan's Island*, talk shows, Soap Operas, and game shows. My mom would leave my brother and I a $1 each per day. In those days you could get a lot for a dollar. The corner store, *"Sam's"* was just three doors down. We would go back and forth buying popsicles, potato chips, and anything else we could fit into our dollar allotment. Sometimes my neighbors and I would buy candy and set up a store on the block, selling candy to people walking by. We were always so creative. Whenever my cousins spent the night, my mom would also leave a dollar for each of them.

Around 5 PM I would take a shower, get dressed for the day, then go outside to play. I would knock on my best friends', Cammy and Kelly's, door to see if they could come out. They couldn't have company nor come outside if their parents weren't home. Sometimes I would knock on some of the other neighbor's doors over on Oakdale or 23rd Streets. I never really ventured too far away from my block.

When I'd see my mom driving down the street after work, I'd chase her car. My uncle and aunt were always present and sat on the porch, watching everyone come and go. My best-friends (we called each other cousins), who lived across the street, were able to come out as soon as their mom, Ms. Cynthia, got home. The rest of the evening, all of the kids came together to run up and down the street. It was the same every day during the summer months.

During the school year, on Friday nights, as soon as I arrived to spend the weekend, I would take my clothes into the house and immediately go across the street to Cammy and Kelly's house. We made up commercials and dance steps to different songs. Later we invited our mothers for Mother's Day and performed *Head to Toe* by Lisa Lisa and Cult Jam. We were then asked to perform it for others in the neighborhood.

We soon realized we were in demand (jokingly) so we continued making up other dances. The next performance was *Lost in Emotion* by Lisa Lisa and Cult Jam. We made up lots of dances though eventually the fire went out and we disbanded. I say this jokingly but I think we may have been on to something and should perhaps have gotten a manager. During the summer of 1984, Kelly and I put on talent shows while my older cousin was the judge. Kelly lip-synched *What's Love Got to Do with It?* by Tina Turner and I always did the same with *Dear Lover* by Teena Marie. Performing has always been a part of my life one way or another.

Kelly was only five when much of this was going on. During the first half of 1983 I was eight. But as we got older, she would say, "the summer of '83 was the best summer!" Again, she was only five – so how much could she actually remember? That was always just so funny to us. That summer, in addition to all of the other games we played, Cammy, Kelly, and I would often go over to Ms. Miller's house. We relayed all the neighborhood gossip to her and we'd sit and talk to her for hours. She would give us *Jello-O Pudding Pops.* It was purely innocent and there was never any funny business. The whole block felt like one big family. I knew I couldn't get into any trouble around there because everybody had their eyes on me (and everyone else). At least that's what it felt like. It was just a warm, family-oriented environment.

I do remember, however, that for some reason, whenever new people came to the neighborhood, I would get into a fight. I remember getting into at least three fights down there. I never got beat up, though. My mom taught me: "don't start 'em, but make sure you finish 'em." So that's what I did. I thought that if I was to grow up in North Philly, I would probably end up having to fight quite often. Although we had great times on the block, I'm sure growing up in North Philly daily wasn't a breeze. Even back when my parents were growing up in that area there were a lot of challenges. I think that is probably true of growing up in most inner cities across the country.

We used to go down *The Parkway* to *Super Sunday*, a yearly event held in the center city that highlighted all types of amusements. I also remember going to the movies at the Cheltenham Mall and downtown. We also used to go to the record and sneaker stores, *The Gallery*, and to the arcades. I got a blue bike for my ninth birthday and then went to the haunted *Brigantine Castle*. There was a large group of us. We were all so scared. I remember my mom putting her arms out in front of us to block us from moving forward, and shouting, "AIN'T NOBODY GOIN' NOWHERE!" We talked about that for years. It was hilarious.

The following year, my cousin threw me a birthday party and invited all the neighborhood kids. My mom had just bought a new couch so my cousin protected it fiercely by taping it off with toilet paper, ensuring no one sat on it. One summer, I hadn't planned on having a party for my birthday but word got out and everyone from camp turned up at my house to celebrate my birthday. I was so surprised. I felt so popular. I have many happy memories of my childhood.

Chapter 2

Navigating

Though my summers in the city were perfect, living with my grandmother during the school year was nearly unbearable. I remember each Sunday while on the way there, we listened to *Butter Ball*, a DJ who played The Oldies on 105.3 WDAS FM. I remember feeling very sad and although I did not have the words to articulate the feelings then. In my clinical studies, I have learned that this is called "alexithymia." This is when one does not have the words for feelings. I can now say that I was feeling and thinking, "here we go, my development would be delayed for yet another week until I left her house again for the weekend." It felt as though my sense of self and respectability were slowly being dismantled piece by piece. My grandmother harassed and provoked me mercilessly. Mark Twain said that the rigorous law of our being is growth. He goes on to assert that we must grow and nothing can prevent it. I didn't understand why it had to be this way; why couldn't I just live in a loving home. I just wanted my mom. I loved her so much.

Living with my grandmother, I did not have the basic needs. According to Abraham Maslow in order for motivation to arise at the next stage, each stage must be satisfied within the individual themselves. I couldn't concentrate on schoolwork; I barely had food and a healthy home/livable environment. Additionally, I didn't feel secure, loved and protected. I always wondered why no one intervened.

Why was I so neglected? We'll look at the word passion (as I will address further in the book). It seems my parents had a very passionate yet unstable relationship. It seems my mom decided to have me, mainly because she saw my dad being such a good father to my older brother; therefore, she wanted to keep him around. Additionally, my dad was getting older and wanted a child. Neither one of them had the internal resources to effectively raise children in a healthy environment; or, at least they didn't want to put forth the effort to cultivate them. They have had so many internal struggles of their own which made it more important for them to get their own needs met as opposed to the full-time responsibility of raising children. That requires putting yourself on the "back burner."

I once heard someone say, "when you meet a man, make sure he was raised up, not just dragged up." I thought, "hmmm, that's me, I was 'dragged' up." I actually remember lugging trash bags of wet clothes that I'd washed at my mom's house on Sundays prior to going up to Elkins Park to my grandmother's. My mom never had a dryer so I would transport them wet then dry them at my grandmother's house. My brother had a nice duffle bag to put his clothes in whereas I had to use trash bag. Those trash bags of wet clothes were extremely heavy for me as a little girl. I remember thinking, "I wish I had a duffle bag like my brother, maybe it would be a little easier for me to carry." Even as a child I knew I was purposely mistreated. I knew all these adults see this. They knew it's wrong. However, I never said anything. I knew they were choosing this behavior and that I was not to even think about challenging them on it. It's sad. I was just a little girl.

I remember that for some reason, one day I stayed behind in North Philly instead of going to my grandmother's. My brother Chris was at my grandparent's. That morning My mom made me a sandwich. I remember it tasted so good and I felt so loved. I just wanted to be cared for that way every day. It should be noted that my goal in disclosing anything in this book is not meant to shame anyone. It's simply my experience from my perspective. Mostly, I believe that people do the best they can with the cards they are dealt, at least as much as their own development allows. No one is perfect and everyone is deserving of love and forgiveness.

My mom eventually told me that her plan had been to get married and have a lot of children and I really don't think she'd ever envisioned being a single parent. Who does? Sometimes being a parent really changes people. I know I changed considerably and in fact, my son thinks that my main mission in life was to raise him. I will speak on my experience raising my son in detail in the chapters to come. In my son's eyes, however, I am nobody but a mom. To highlight this point, I remember watching a movie in which the mom was once a prolific painter. She mentioned this to her kids and they just ran off, laughing, saying, "yeah, right, you're just a mom." She was really hurt and I could totally relate.

My son doesn't realize that before he was born, I was a person with a personality and dreams just like anyone else. You sacrifice a large part of your life for your children. I've spoken with many mothers who've experienced such an identity crisis. Ironically, after denying ourselves many activities and ambitions, by the time we become empty nesters, we experience yet another identity crisis. These phase of life issues that affect empty nesters is real. It is very challenging for some to get back to who they were before they had children.

I digress, however... I went on to the sixth grade in September of 1985. Things continued to be pretty much unbearable at my grandmother's house. I always fought back when she hit me but she harassed me emotionally, mentally, and she abused me physically just because I was there. She treated me like a second-class citizen in that house while she held my brother in such high regard. For example, my brother and I were supposed to alternate days to wash the dishes. He never ended up having to wash them on his day, whereas I HAD to wash them on my day or I would get a beating.

One day, my grandmother tried to force me to wash dishes on my brother's day and I refused so she made me stand in the corner for hours.

One evening my cousin made me spill my hot tea causing me to get a second degree burn on my leg. No one took me to the hospital or the doctor and to make matters worse, I got a beating because the tea had spilled. Another time my brother, my cousin and I were sleeping in the living room and someone was playing with my grandmother's candy dish. She came in and assumed it was me and tried to beat me. I don't remember if it was me who messed with the dish or not but the point is that she didn't care who it was; I was going to get a beating no matter what. She was old and couldn't really hurt me physically but it was that constant feeling of being hated and "tolerated" that hurt the most.

She and my mother would sometimes talk, saying the most disparaging, untrue things about me in my presence. I had to grow up in those conditions. I never thought I was the problem though because outside of that house I felt somewhat accepted and happy. The treatment I experienced was unjust and abusive day in and day out for years while I lived there. It was just so sad. There is no excuse for this maltreatment; however, thinking back, it was not my grandmother's job to raise me or any of her grandchildren for that matter. In frustration one day, she said, "I'm only doing this because I promised my

husband that I would let you kids stay here!"
Nonetheless, I still feel that God has had his eyes on me through it all. He has a purpose for each one of us and he will see it through. Jeremiah 1:12 tells us that he is keeping his eye on us to ensure that His will is done through us.

Chapter 3

Extra-Curricular

School was an outlet for me while I lived at my grandmother's and therefore, I rarely missed a day. It was a bright and nurturing place where I found safety and food. According to Kilka and Herrenkohl (2015), school and peer acceptance are influential in determining the level of resilience in children who are maltreated and/or neglected at home. While I didn't always feel like I fit in at school, there was definitely some level of safety and acceptance.

I went to a couple of meetings for *The Brownies* early on in elementary school and in sixth grade I was on the track team. I always loved being involved, but my life was so unstable I could never completely commit to anything as I didn't have anyone to take me to the scheduled events and meetings.

In fifth grade, my teacher, Ms. Derr did an experiment with our class for Black History Month. She separated us by last names. Everyone with the last name beginning A through N stood on one side of the room; and everyone with the last name beginning O through Z stood on another side of the classroom. The first group received privileged treatment whereas the second group received second class treatment.

I remember how irate the second group became throughout the day. And I remember looking down on them wondering why they were so angry and thinking (just that fast), that there must be something wrong with them for them to be treated in such a way. I also remember a slight feeling of hurt at seeing how the others were being treated. My teacher was teaching us firsthand about White privilege and Black oppression. We got to understand how it feels to be privileged and those in the other group got to empathize with what it feels like to be oppressed. Unfortunately, there were only four Black kids in my class and ironically, with the exception of mine, their last names all fell into the underprivileged group.

Reflecting on that exercise today, it is even more evident to me how compassionate and thoughtful a teacher Ms. Derr was. Because she'd probably realized how marginalized I already was and because I was only one of four Black kids in the class, she chose to put me in the privileged group knowing that, unfortunately, the other Black students, who already knew what it felt like to be marginalized would have to go through it again for this experiment. She could easily have left me in the underprivileged group but had decided that she didn't want to do that to me as she may have seen that I had probably already gone through enough. I'm not sure if this was the case but it wouldn't surprise me. I remember her always being very patient and taking the extra time to help me out whenever she felt I was struggling

I remember sixth grade we had a track meet at *The University of Pennsylvania*. My dad was there looking for me. He was so proud of me. But I wasn't there. No one had taken me to the meet. The kids came to school the following Monday and told me he'd been there. I was extremely embarrassed because it seemed that everyone else's life was so much more in order than mine.

I had the same teacher in sixth grade as I did in the fourth. She was not as kind and patient as Ms. Derr though. In fact, I almost failed sixth grade, but I pulled myself up and started getting As and Bs. To me, this was a huge accomplishment because I was still unkempt (masked by Liz Claiborne clothes from *Strawbridge & Clothier* and *John Wannamaker's*), malnourished, neglected, and abused at home. Some mothers see their daughters as an extension of themselves, and if the daughter looks good on the outside, so does she (McBride, 2008). Somehow however, I still managed to pass my classes in spite of inadequate supervision at home and no proper school supplies.

I remember lying in bed one night while at my grandmother's when a thought popped into my head: "no one cares." It was true, really...but this thought combined with another thought I'd had in second grade (which I will discuss later): "I control my life," are thoughts that were set up in my childhood that basically, guided me for the rest of my life. While the thought that "no one cares" may have actually been the enemy speaking, it was my experience at that time. In the sixth grade, however, my dad noticed that I was becoming emaciated and took me to the doctor's. He was concerned about my weight. I started taking vitamins. They seemed to have worked. It's hard to tell because we still didn't have much food at my grandmother's.

As an adult you can challenge your negative thoughts, thinking of all of the contradictions; but in your formative years as a little kid, you grow up in certain conditions that could ultimately determine the trajectory of your life. The foundational years contribute greatly to the wiring of your brain and how one's core beliefs are formed. I cannot stress enough how important it is to bring your child(ren) up in a nurturing and loving environment so they can develop correctly, at least mentally and emotionally.

In January of 1986, the other two sixth grade classes joined our class to watch the Space Shuttle Challenger take off. I clearly remember the look on the teachers' faces when something suddenly went wrong. I didn't know what was going on. They all looked stunned. My teacher turned off the TV, the other classes left, and we were told to go back to our seats. I remember seeing a lot of smoke on TV but it didn't register that the rocket had blown up just seconds after take-off.

I graduated in June of 1986 and headed for Junior High. To prepare us, we watched movies about staying away from drugs and other teenage antics. My teacher stressed the importance of writing in cursive as it would be important when taking notes. We were extremely sheltered. We were schooled on how fast we'd need to transfer between classes, including stopping at our lockers. This scared me more than anything, but they were just trying to prepare us. My academic experience was wholesome, welcoming, bright, and nurturing, pretty much from first through twelfth grade.

In September of 1986, I started seventh grade at Abington Junior High School. Junior High was uneventful, for the most part. I remember going to the long-awaited dances I'd heard my brother and older cousin raving so much about. Although I was content, for the first year, I felt like a tiny fish in a big pond but eventually, I adjusted.

Kids at McKinley, sometimes, made fun of my broken English early on. For example, in third grade, I remember someone making fun of the way I mispronounced ask, saying "axe" instead. I quickly learned to articulate and pronounce my words correctly. This was mainly accomplished unconsciously by osmosis. However, whenever I went to North Philly, I had to switch it up real fast. I tried hard not to speak so properly. My Philly accent came back quickly but over time, spending more of my life in the suburbs, I couldn't really hide it much longer. Kids in North Philly, said I talked like a "White girl." However, the same was true with some of the other kids at Abington Junior High who weren't from McKinley either. Because I was from McKinley, some of the kids from other area schools in Abington Township and most of the Black girls would say I was a "White girl." The whole township is predominantly White but some of the other elementary schools had more Black students than McKinley. It was strange because McKinley is older and the homes are not even as nice as the ones in other neighborhoods throughout the township. I think the kids from McKinley, had the rep of having more money back then, simply because we were way on the other side of the township and our school may have had a higher White to Black student ratio; but not because we had more money (my household definitely didn't) or nice homes; not by a long shot.

Chapter 4

Turning Point

When I started seventh grade at Abington Junior High School in September 1986, *The Show* by Dougie Fresh and Slick Rick and *Eric B. for president* by Eric and B. and Rakim were hit songs. I remember feeling really intimidated in such a big school, compared to being in elementary School. Most of the people I went to elementary school with were no longer in any of my classes. Most of us were split up, it seems. The feeling of unfamiliarity loomed over me and I didn't feel comfortable with these new students.

I would reunite with my friends from elementary school at after-school events and outside of school. I remember having my first detention in seventh grade and being scared to death. We had to sit in the cafeteria for an hour after school. To this day I still remember the proctor's face. He was so scary. I was always either talking or singing in class which is why between seventh to eleventh grade I often had to "serve" detention. I ended up with five detentions by the end of seventh grade alone. I used to hate detention because we had to get on the 4:15 bus, meaning we wouldn't get home until at least 5:00 PM. I guess we were supposed to complete our homework in detention. I never did.

My life changed in March of 1987. The show *Rags to Riches* aired. My heart fluttered. It was what I had been searching for without even knowing it. It was the answer to my dreams. I began recording every show and watching every episode ad nauseam, remembering and reciting every line and every word to every song. I thought, "I don't want to do anything other than this." In my early years, I performed all the time. I even played the character "Tessie" in *Annie* in a small play we staged in class. Later, I saw a performance of *Annie* at the *City Line Dinner Theater*. I loved it there. I have always loved musical theater. I honestly can't say that as an adult I would want to perform it but as a kid that's all I wanted to do.

Because of so much instability in my childhood, I eventually longed for the stability of a regular 9-5 but was pursuing my other goals and dreams as an adjunct to that. My mom even said that she could hear my voice above the rest when singing in the chorus at my sixth-grade graduation. My music teacher also mentioned that my singing stood out in music class.

I believe a parent should observe their child so they can know which way to steer them. It's important to support them in activities which they automatically gravitate towards. When you see that a child has a talent or affinity for something, it's important to guide that child in that direction. Based on all the performing and leading that I'd done up to that point, an attentive parent would've known how to guide me. And my mother knew, she just didn't bother to follow through with the support. I remember my mom saying that she was going to sign me up for *Freedom Theater,* a performing arts theater, but she never did. However, I've learned that your dreams never leave you and thankfully, many acting and performing classes were yet to come.

I was devastated when they took *Rags to Riches* off the air in 1988. It only lasted two seasons. I believe that show was somewhat of a savior for me. It kept me occupied, my mind off my troubles at home and off of the boys too. The recordings kept me going, until ninth grade when started to like boys. However, I was so busy with extra-curricular activities inside and outside of school that I didn't have much time to give them any serious thought.

When I was in the eighth grade, I was reunited with the person who would become my best-friend throughout my high school years, Kerri Conner (now Kerri Conner-Matchett). We went to elementary school together. Kerri invited me to the 9th grade cheerleading try-outs, and I made the team. It was there that I felt I found my tribe. I found my people. During ninth grade, in addition to being a cheerleader, I was on student council, intramural gymnastics (our school didn't have a gymnastics team), public speaking, and any other activity I could think of. I had found myself. I was growing into the person I wanted to be. I was thriving.

I even ran for class secretary though I thought I was signing up for something else! I didn't even want to but I ran anyway without putting any effort into my campaign. Though I won the primaries, I lost the general election, which was fine by me because I didn't really want to be class secretary anyways. Besides, the person to whom I lost was an amazing student that everyone admired.

The summer before ninth grade my dad signed me up for a summer enrichment program at *Temple University* called AFNA (I don't recall what AFNA stood for). I loved it because I felt like someone cared enough about me to set expectations for me. During the weekend my dad signed my younger siblings and me up for acting lessons and gymnastics. We had headshots taken and met with casting directors. I remember practicing signing my autograph. While in tenth grade, my agent wanted me to audition for *Rocky V*. Unfortunately, at that point I was heading off track and my grades were slipping so the agency wouldn't allow me to audition.

I flourished in ninth grade, however. I knew who I was, where I was going, and what I wanted to do. My dad and his other family had moved to Philly the year before. He and I were both tired of the living conditions at my grandmother's. He had listened to my lamentations for years. He and I spoke of me ceasing to live with my grandmother and moving in with him. I expressed to him my desire to go to the *High School for*

Creative and Performing Arts in Philadelphia (*CAPA*). I knew that all I had to do was mention my desires to my dad and it was as good as done.

He took my mom to court to get custody of me when I was in the tenth grade and the following year, I stopped living at my grandmother's house. My dad fought for me on several occasions. He really wanted me with him. I know it broke his heart that he never got to have that long term. He really did want the best for me.

Tryouts for the tenth-grade cheerleading team were held in ninth grade. Because I didn't think I would be at Abington during my tenth-grade year, I didn't bother to try out. Tenth grade came and I was back at Abington at which time I continued to live with my grandmother. I wasn't sure what had happened but my dad wasn't able to get me into CAPA. I say my dad didn't "get me into" because, as previously mentioned, all I had to do was mention a desire to my dad and it was done. But something had obviously fallen through because I stayed where I was. I was in my comfort zone, however so it wasn't so bad.

The Abington school district is designed in such a way that all seven elementary school students funnel into Abington Junior High and from there into Abington Senior High School. I was nestled in my little cocoon and was familiar with everything and everybody. I had a little apprehension about going to CAPA, anyway. I was more of a suburban girl at that point. CAPA was in

Center City. Also, while I loved singing and dancing, I'd always struggled with what I might do for my CAPA audition. Would my audition be good enough? I suppose if I'd pushed harder or looked into it further, something would have materialized but at the time, I didn't believe in myself enough. Either way, I found out that my dad and his other family had been going through their own issues.

There was really no ideal place for me to go as a child short of going away to boarding school, which was never discussed. Looking back, had it been an option, it may have been the most stable and healthy environment for me. In any case, *Abington* was very prolific and well-suited to meet all student's interests; I could have signed up for theater there and still made it to where I wanted to go. I was a horrible reader in primary and secondary school simply because I didn't read very much. It sounds simple but if you want to be a good reader, you simply must read a lot, which I discovered much later. Because of this, I was too intimidated to participate in theater at *Abington*. Instead, I took Radio/TV, acting, cinema, and chorus classes, along with my regular academic classes.

In the tenth grade, I began taking part in mild anti-social behaviors. I started drinking "forties" in the park with others after-school. Sometimes, we even drank on our way to school and I went to school drunk more than once. On some weekends it was the same. I didn't like the taste of beer; I just drank it for the high jinks of it all. I even got into the occasional fight. I was really heading in the wrong direction.

Since I hadn't tried out for tenth-grade cheerleading, consequently I had nothing productive to do after-school while all of my good friends were busy with extra-curricular activities. I hadn't planned on being at Abington after ninth-grade, but I clearly hadn't really planned to go to *CAPA* either. Earl Nightingale in *The Strangest Secret*, states that when you don't steer your ship, you'll end up on the wrong course, a derelict (paraphrasing). I love what Maya Angelou said in *Oprah Winfrey's Master Class*; on speaking about making your way in the world, she said, "try to live your life in a way that you will not regret years of useless virtue, inertia and timidity..." This is a good reminder that we are all here for a purpose and not to waste our time wandering around aimlessly. Get about the work of fulfilling your purpose on this planet as soon as you can.

I had a best friend from Philly that I'd met at an overnight camp. We used to get into mischief together and she began urging me to try sex. I didn't want to and wasn't ready nor was I interested. However, I was bored and had nothing productive to do after-school. I'd begun listening to *N.W.A.* and *Eazy-E*. That's when I learned that an idle mind is truly the enemy's playground.

I began experimenting with a neighborhood boy named Jake as he wasn't doing anything after school either. I didn't find sex enjoyable at the time, it was simply something to do. Call it boredom or experimentation, this behavior continued for the rest of the school year and into the summer months between summer school and overnight camp. I had been going to overnight camps with my siblings since third grade all the way to the summer before eleventh grade.

In September 1990 I started 11th grade. Thankfully, I'd been smart enough during my 10th grade year to try out for cheerleading just in case I returned to *Abington*. So, that year I was on the 11th grade cheerleading team. I felt like my life was getting back on track though I was still getting drunk and going to parties with my friends. After all of the abuse and neglect I'd endured, it seems my self-image was beginning to be reflected in my life choices.

I began dating my first serious boyfriend in the 11th grade. I'll call him Sam. I finally felt a sense of normalcy. I thought, "I've finally got it right." I was as happy as I'd ever been. Our relationship was pure. We'd known each other since eighth grade and we were friends. For whatever reason, two weeks prior to us making our relationship official, I had relations with Jake. I was coming from cheerleading practice and getting off the 5:15 bus. At that time, I was living with my mother and commuting back-and-forth between North Philly to Abington every day.

It was dark by the time I got to the bus stop to go home to North Philly when I realized that I needed to go to go to the bathroom. Against my better judgment I asked Jake if I could use the bathroom at his house. I had a bad feeling when I asked him and something told me, "don't talk to him...just get on the bus and go home." But I didn't listen to my inner voice. It was dark and at least an hour and a half ride on public transportation before I'd get to my mom's. We had relations and then I got on the bus to go home to North Philly...

The entire time Sam and I were dating I was pregnant, only I didn't know it; or I should say, I didn't realize the seriousness of the situation. In my 16-year-old brain I honestly could not foresee that a baby could actually come out of me. I came to realize later that this type of denial is not uncommon. Adolescents generally cannot see that far into the future. They simply don't have the capacity to as their brains are not yet fully formed.

My life became such a contradiction because I was happy and finally felt like I was on the right track. At the same time, I was in complete denial about what was going on with me physiologically. Over the next months, I completely suppressed the fact that I was with child. In fact, I remember my dad taking me to get my prom dress and feeling so beautiful even though my stomach was sticking out. My dad laughed adoringly and said, "Karima, you're getting fat." Sam's father paid for the limo and we went to the junior prom. For once, I was sooo happy. I finally felt whole and my life seemed "right."

Sometime in December of 1990, while I was standing in My mom's kitchen, she reached over and felt my stomach then asked me if I was pregnant. I responded with: "not by Sam." At which point she simply stormed up the steps. I was the child that was to be seen and not heard so even though I would sometimes go into my mom's room and sit next to her wanting to talk, she'd simply dismiss me, telling me to get out of her room and go wash the dishes or something.

I wanted someone to help me with my situation but I was never encouraged to speak up for myself so I didn't have the words to effectively approach her. I tried to tell her in several ways and on many occasions and it seems that as a mother she should've intuitively picked up on the cues that something was going on with me but she didn't want to. Some have suggested that she in fact knew what was going on but subconsciously wanted me to have a baby. I now understand that sometimes parents know the truth about a situation, but may not "have time to deal with it," so things get swept under the rug.

I've had to have many uncomfortable talks with my son. It's hard, but you have to do it. As a single mom raising a boy, I even had to bring up discussions about sex and the circumstances of his life with him. It was pretty uncomfortable but I knew I had to do it. Other than my dad, no one respected me enough to hold me accountable for anything. As a result, I worked really hard to make him proud of me. I never wanted to disappoint him and in fact I wanted to weep whenever I thought I may have. When a parent sets high expectations for a child, that child rises to the occasion. The opposite is also true: low expectations cause children to underperform and live below their potential. Believing in your child is paramount to helping him or her develop self-esteem and courage. Your belief in them fuels their belief in themselves.

When I was in the tenth grade, my older sister approached me and asked me if she needed to take me to *Planned Parenthood*. I didn't want to take birth control because I thought only "loose" girls did so and I didn't see myself as that type of person. I told her no. As the year went on my stomach started to grow even though I was still cheerleading. I hid the pregnancy by wearing a white windbreaker almost every day, even when it started to get really warm outside. People at school questioned me about my jacket but I denied any claims of pregnancy and brushed off the fact that it was too hot to be wearing a windbreaker, telling them that I was cold. It became ridiculous after a while. There was no way I could be cold on some days. Well, somehow, Sam found out about my condition and broke up with me. We were both devastated. That summer I gave birth to my son...I was just 16 years old.

I really wanted to give my son up for adoption. As previously mentioned, I was a child who'd been trained to be seen and not heard. I couldn't openly or effectively express anything I was going through, except to my dad. I always felt that I could talk to him. He made me feel validated. However, when it came to my pregnancy, I don't think I knew how to broach the subject with him. As my stomach began to get bigger, however, I somehow built up the nerve to take action. I contacted several adoption agencies and I was actually in talks with one of them. Once my dad found out, he and my mom got me on the phone to discuss the situation. I finally got a chance to tell them of my plan. My mom was initially on board, but my dad was not having any parts of giving his grandson up for adoption (we knew the sex by that time). I heard my dad tell my mom, "don't let her give my grandson up for adoption." To which my mom replied, "I'm not." So that was that.

I kept thinking, "what in the world am I going to do?" I felt helpless and hopeless. I felt as if my life was over. This was traumatic for me. Trauma in and of itself "changes the plot." My family wasn't a family I wanted to bring a child into because of how they'd treated me. I also knew I wouldn't have any real support but my parents simply would not allow me to give him up for adoption.

I now have to live with Allender's (2005) assertion of the orphan child as it pertains to my son (an me, in some ways, perhaps). He speaks of how a boy without a father has a life with a slowed my momentum of meaning, possibly accelerating off course at tragic speeds. He also speaks on how a boy without a father has no protection, and that he may find it challenging to establish an identity. I have seen this in my son (and in some ways – myself) and it's a horrible thing to watch. I believe he is slowly getting through this phase but his teenage and early adult years were extremely difficult for him.

Having a child at age 16 that I had to raise without a responsible father, and later having to deal with the alienation that comes with having a rebellious child, have deeply shaped my life. Though it made me more reflective, it also made me more isolated. I got through it, but not without having to deal with the loneliness of single motherhood at a very young age. None of this is my son's fault but there is no doubt he felt my struggle. Children pick up on everything. They don't necessarily have the words to express how they feel, instead they tend to exhibit behaviors that demonstrate their emotions.

Allender writes about the "widow shame," which I identify with. I am the "non-promiscuous single" he refers to. I am single because I have not been chosen. However, I recently read a post on social media that stated, "Being single doesn't mean you're undesirable; it means you know your worth and you are waiting for someone who is worthy" (and I might add…who also sees your worth). However, Allender goes on to describe how hard it is to attend parties, sit at church, and go shopping knowing that no one has committed to me. There is a shame connected to being a single parent, especially as a Christian woman, which is how I identified for a long time. I now identify simply as a "believer in the Word of God."

Furthermore, Allender proposes that in the presence of love, we are rightly named and it is there that we find our story. I never imagined as a child that my life would be filled with so many obstacles. I know that having a child at 16 changed the trajectory of my life, but I pray that God is not done with me yet. He places the desire in us to seek love and He said that it is not good for man to be alone so all I can do is continue being the best person I can be and continue asking, seeking, and knocking, and prayerfully God's will shall be done.

Being a caring mother (or parent) is an instinctual thing; at least it was for me. Although, when I was 16, I didn't want to be a mother, I saw this little boy being rolled into my room then they sat him next to my bed. I looked at him and his eyes were big and wide open. He was breathtaking. Sadly though, I felt no connection to him. I didn't want a child at that age and I definitely didn't want a child by that person... I didn't pick my son up that day, but I couldn't help but notice his beautiful eyes. Everyone said he looked mixed. To me, he looked like a little Eskimo. He was literally the cutest baby I'd ever seen. One could not help but to fall in love with a baby that beautiful.

A few days later I took him home. I remember jumping out of the car as if to say, "this isn't going to hold me down!" I can't remember if I brought him into the house or if someone else did, but I do remember feeling embarrassed. I just never saw myself as a teen my mom. That was in July of 1991.

I went to cheerleading camp at the end of August that year. Again, I was not ready to be a parent which I told my parents in so many ways and on multiple occasions. I couldn't help but feel frustration over the fact that these people, who didn't even raise me, got to make decisions for my life, thus creating overwhelming obstacles for me and for future generations. It wasn't right but I did the best I could with the choices that were made FOR me. I tried really hard to do the right thing for myself and my son.

For the most part, besides the fact that I now had a baby, my 12th grade year was uneventful. When I left the house to go from N. Philly to Abington it was so early that Matthew would still be asleep so my mom would take him to the lady's house down the street. Then, I would pick him up when I came home from school.

That year, two of my friends, my cousin, and I had a big party at the Germantown YMCA. We handed out flyers all around the city and the surrounding areas. We rented the hall and charged people an cover fee. At the end of the night, we paid the DJ and kept the profits.

We were pretty excited when we walked away with about $300 each that evening. My cousin, friends, and I celebrated by getting seafood at *Sam's Clams* off of South Street. For a moment there, I thought that hosting events and parties was what I wanted to do with my life. The money just came so fast and easy. At 17 that was a lot of money for one night. I wasn't able to continue cheerleading too far into my senior year because I had to get home to my son. I finished school that summer and went to college in September of 1992.

For the first two years of my son's life, I was not emotionally present. It wasn't that I was cold-hearted, I just didn't have a connection. I once heard a well-known talk show host and a famous R & B singer talking about this phenomenon. I felt they were the only ones who could relate to me in this respect. I went away to college when I was 18. I stayed on campus all week then came home on weekends. My son pretty much bonded with my mom during the first three years of his life.

I didn't do very well in school so I was only accepted into Cheyney University and one other state school though I knew I needed to go to a Historically Black College and University (HBCU). I didn't really want to go to Cheyney, but I definitely wanted to get away from my family. There just seemed to be one obstacle after another. I needed to breathe. It was as if my mom was intent on piling up obstacles in my life, purposely making my life difficult. I did appreciate the HBCU's influence on my life however. After being in predominately White institutions from first to twelfth grades, I felt I'd lost my identity and really needed to attend an HBCU. I felt my identity as an African-American "quickened" during my time there, although, until recently, I had never really felt "Black enough" in social situations.

My son continued to be the most beautiful baby I'd ever seen. I continued to be physically but not emotionally present. I get the sense that some on my mom's side of the family saw our lack of bonding as my fault, and that I was someone without the capacity to love. However, they choose not to see truth about the whole situation. Cognitive dissonance. That spirit looms over me to this day.

I remember a couple of weeks after my son turned one, I came home from work to find that my brother had cut my son's hair without asking me first. My baby had the most beautiful curly hair. I was not ready to see him look like a little boy. That was traumatic in and of itself. Any mother can relate to this. To this day, whenever I think about my baby's face without all of his hair I am saddened.

On my maternal side I was always made to feel invisible, invalidated, and disregarded. Most times my position as my son's mother was just not respected. One reason for my brother's actions could have been the lack of parental affection we grew up with. When I was 19, I started studying early childhood education. That's when I began to get serious about raising my child. I studied early childhood education so I knew, at least by the book, what a child needed for proper development. I thought, "I'm going to rise to the occasion and learn from others' mistakes." My son was stunningly gorgeous and smart. My dad and I took him to *Screen Test USA* to get pictures taken then sent them off to casting agencies. He went on a few auditions and walked in a few fashion shows but he wasn't really interested in that world at that time.

I often tell my son that he saved my life. Though it may not have seemed that way to me in the beginning, having him was definitely a watershed moment for me. It is because of him that I started to take myself and my life more seriously. I had to be there for him. If it wasn't for him, I wouldn't have gotten serious about my education. He made me determined to graduate from college and get a decent job so I could provide for us.

Life was hard trying to raise my little boy while living with my mom, but I persisted. For a while he was going to a neighborhood daycare. When he was three, I shopped around to find a more quality day care for him. I finally settled on a private Christian school called Timothy Academy. He thrived there. When he was four, however, I received a "Section 8" voucher. I was twenty-one and so happy to finally be out from under my family and raise my son on my own.

Prior to graduating from undergrad, representatives from Prince George's County in Maryland came to my college to recruit teachers. I thought very seriously about my son and I moving to Maryland but I just didn't know how I would do it completely alone. In addition to the issues I was having with my family, our neighborhood in North Philly was changing. On two separate occasions bullets flew into my mom's house. One time a bullet flew right past me as my son and I were sitting in the living room. So, my son and I moved to Bala Cynwyd, a very affluent area right outside of Philadelphia. We were finally happy, still a bit isolated, but happy. Needless to say, I was elated to get out of North Philly.

My son went to day care at Lower Merion High School, the same place where Kobe Bryant attended high school. Then for kindergarten and first grade, he went to the neighborhood school, Merion Elementary, where he continued to flourish. I volunteered in his classrooms and attended his sporting events. He was in basketball, track, and karate, just to name a few. By this time, I loved being a mom and raising my son. He continued to be the most amazing little boy. I took great pride in caring for him. His first-grade teacher told me, "I can tell you spend a lot of time with him; he's very advanced."

He had his own room in our nice, clean apartment and we found a church that we attended together. It was there that I got baptized. I was just 21 years old. Every community my son and I lived in together was nice. He could just be a kid riding his bike around the neighborhood. I had this as a child and I wanted it for him because I knew how important it was for his development; to freely explore his neighborhood and just be a kid.

My commute from our apartment to school was shorter than from my mom's house to school. My baby would be at school from 6 am to 6 pm. He went to before-school care, regular school, and then after-school programs. I was really happy though. My grandmother came over for a week to watch my son when he had pneumonia. I had finally earned her respect. As I was leaving the apartment one day, she patted me on the back and said, "you're a good mom."

The apartment complex came under new management and they no longer accepted section 8 so we could no longer afford to live there and had to move back in with my mom. I graduated that May and began working. I transferred my son to my former elementary school in Elkins Park, McKinley Elementary, as soon as he finished first grade at Merion. McKinley was a lot further from my mom's so there were times when my son had to stay the night with my grandmother.

We had been doing quite well until we were forced to re-unite with my family again. My son did okay in school at McKinley in the beginning. I was still involved in his education; however, he wasn't really involved in too many activities at his new school. Since the time I had attended McKinley to my son's attendance, the atmosphere seemed to have changed. Perhaps as a child I hadn't really noticed, but now that my son was enrolled there, I soon realized that the racial tension was so thick you could cut it with a knife. Plus, my son was not being treated well by my grandmother. I knew this.

It wasn't so much that I was repeating a cycle but more that I wanted my son to go to a good school and he could no longer stay at Merion. I looked at private schools but I couldn't afford them and was unable to get scholarships. I worked in North Philly where my mom lived and my son went to school in Elkins Park. For a while I drove back and forth every day. I thought, "what harm could my grandmother do in that short amount of time?" It turns out, that was all the time she needed to mistreat him. In September of 1998, my car died. I then, took the bus every day to go see him. I felt horrible about it. My mom wouldn't let me use her car to go visit my son. I feel like she wanted so badly for me to repeat the cycle of having someone else be responsible for raising my child.

In November of 1998 I was able to purchase my own car with my own money. By then, I was 24 years old. I bought a *Nissan 200SX* and I loved it. I could now take my son to school every day. However, he would sometimes still have to stay the night at my grandmother's. In March of 1999, my mom poured dirty mop water on my bed and kicked me and my son out in the cold because my brother refused to wash the dishes. This protection of the male child could have been a cultural thing. In many cultures the women protect the male child more than the female one. Perhaps they were deemed as the more valuable offspring at one point in time.

Anyway, my son and I went to live at my cousin's apartment in Cheltenham, closer to my son's school. That's when he started having problems in school. I got a report that he'd urinated on himself on the playground; which he later denied, stating that he was behaving mischievously. I was heart-broken nonetheless. I was in love with this little boy by this time and tried so hard to provide for and protect him.

Growing up, my son had a new interest every year. When he was two, he loved *Barney the Dinosaur*. When he was three it was *The Lion King*. When he was four, he loved *The Power Rangers.* When he was six, he was into *Crazy Bones* and *Beanie Babies*. In addition, I would get surprises whenever I washed his clothes. He always had ants, rocks, and worms in his pockets. One of my cousins jokingly called him "Nature Boy." When he turned seven, he started to love video games and his *Game Boy*. At eight he got into wrestling and *Pokemon* which lasted for a couple of years until he started to play basketball and *PlayStation* games.

When he was 11 years old, he loved to rap and he started performing and this is what stuck. He literally excelled at everything he did, even academically. He got straight A's on everything until about the third of fourth grade. Subconsciously, I wanted to see a B somewhere. I wanted to be sure teachers were not over-looking him. I was actually relieved when he began getting B's in third grade. He has always been really smart and it's not that I didn't think that he could get A's, it's just that I wanted him to be challenged. He was well prepared for school though and all of his teachers said so. I always got so many compliments about him from the teachers and the other parents.

In September of 1999, my son and I moved into another apartment in Northeast Philadelphia. My sister had an apartment just around the corner and we were finally happy again. He and I lived in that apartment from the time he was eight until he was 12. He had become my pride and joy. I worked hard to give him everything I'd never had. It wasn't easy, and there were times where I worked two and three jobs.

One day a fax came through at work offering discount tickets to *Disney World*. I took my chances and purchased them. We had to sit through a timeshare presentation but as a result, we were able to attend four parks (*Magic Kingdom, Epcot, Universal Studios,* and *MGM Studios*). To me, he was a perfect little boy and I expected the best out of him. I remember us driving home one evening, after I picked him up from my grandmother's, and telling him, "you are great and to whom much is given much will be expected." Those were not just empty words. I honestly believed that from the bottom of my heart.

For a long time, I wished I'd had him later in life so that I could've given him the life he truly deserved. Though it wasn't all bad, no kid deserves to go through the hard times he went through. There were plenty of times though where we cuddled, and I would have to lay down with him in order for him to fall asleep until he was about four. He made me breakfast for Mother's Day and wrote me poems. He loved his mom. Although he had his own room, until he was about eight or nine years old, he often slept in my bed. It was purely innocent. That's just where he was comfortable sometimes; and after all, I had done the same with my mom.

I recall having to take him to the barbershop to get his hair cut. I hated it. I felt like all of the men were staring at me which made me feel really uncomfortable. I was so relieved when he got old enough that I could just drop him off then pick him up afterwards. I had to spend about $12 I didn't have every week but I wanted him to be presentable. After a while I watched the barbers carefully, bought clippers, and started cutting his hair myself, thus saving money and the embarrassment of having to go into those barber shops as a young single woman.

When my son was in the fourth grade I came to his class and delivered a lesson on the African-American contributions to America. The list was so long that the lesson lasted at least an hour. I did this because my son, who was the only African-American in his class, was coming home in tears nearly every day because of the way he was being treated. It was especially hard during Black History Month when he kept getting stares which made him feel very uncomfortable. So, I came in and I did a lesson on all of the African-American contributions to America. It was a really good, interactive lesson filled with visual aids and lots of hands-on learning. I brought in as many real-life examples as I could, including an ironing board and fire-extinguisher. The students were very engaged in the lesson.

Chapter 5

Intimacy Vs. Isolation

When we were both 21, Sam and I got back together. After all, we were each other's first love. We were best friends and it was pure love, some may say puppy love. But it was pure. We stayed together, off and on, until we were 25. He really loved my son. And my son loved him. However, between the time we were 16 until age 25 Sam had grown and matured tremendously. He was becoming self-actualized, whereas I was growing as a mom with no real identity other than that. We had both changed so much. My social life had suffered and therefore, that part of my development had been stunted. Sam on the other hand had grown into a well-rounded person. Things were just not the same. By the time we were about 25, he barely came over any more and we never went out during the day.

He really didn't want to be with me though I thought he still loved me. He couldn't quite get over his first love, as was the case with me. Emotionally, I thought he loved me but developmentally he was not ready to be a husband and a father (nor should he have been) and I was just not the same lighthearted, jovial, fun person I'd been in high school. Knowing how much he and my son loved each other, it broke my heart when I realized that we couldn't stay together. I don't think he ever truly forgave me for what happened in high school and I know I never forgave myself. Because I knew deep down that Sam no longer wanted to make a life with me, I broke up with him essentially to set him free. I felt like he was just too good for me and I didn't want to ruin his life. He had way too much potential.

In graduate school we read a book called *Truth be Told* by Dan B. Allender (2005). He writes of people who have had so many tragedies in life, that they don't know where one ends and the other begins. Sometimes I feel that is true with my life. Recently, I had likened my life to a quarterback with the ball, heading for a touchdown. I got to a place where I wondered why my life had been a series of events designed to destroy me. Those who raise us, play a part in setting events in motion in our lives. I wasn't always successful at it, but I definitely made every effort to do better with my son.

I understand that people may see a divide when they look at me and my son's relationship. I believe, there is a chasm there, however, I did not and would not purposely choose to put a child or myself in such a difficult situation. I personally don't know anyone else who has had this experience nor does my son. I tried to do the right thing by placing him in a better situation, but I was often not supported in that choice. What was I to do? Ship him off to be mistreated by other family members so they could say "she's just like her mother, she's not raising her own child either." and other disparaging things? Or should I "suck it up" and do the right thing and take responsibility for my actions? I chose to do the latter. Unfortunately, my son and I still feel a gap in our relationship to this day. It's not fair that anyone should have to go through life feeling void of a truly authentic, warm, loving, nurturing, long-lasting, consistent mother-child relationship. We've had to work to attain that. Some people have noticed the tension between us which is why there has been so much interference and continued disruption. Sometimes I feel that he truly doesn't realize that I'm his mother.

Chapter 6

Growing up can be a Pain

When my son was 12, we moved to Glenside, another section of the Abington Township. He had graduated from McKinley and would now be going to the Junior High School, Abington Junior High. Only now he no longer had to lie about where he lived. I had to do that growing up and I vowed that my kids would never have to have that burden. In doing that, one just feels like their whole life is a lie. But my son now lived in the township. Unfortunately, though things were looking up; as previously mentioned, he had begun to have some problems adjusting in school.

The day we moved to Glenside that August of 2004, Matthew wasn't with me. Instead, he was with his paternal grandmother that weekend. They had a very close relationship. I didn't want him to have to deal with the stresses of moving. I wanted him to enjoy himself and be loved and comfortable so I let him stay with his grandmother all weekend. In everything I did, I tried hard to nurture him, put his needs first, and give him the best life I could.

He started the school year at Abington Junior High that September. I'd hoped that he'd have no more obstacles, but having gone to Abington myself, I knew that the kids who lived in the apartments where we lived, or really any apartments for that matter always seemed to be on the fringe of the social groups at Abington. They didn't seem to fit in as well as the students whose relatives were homeowners. It didn't even matter if the houses were owned by their grandparents instead of their parents, they had more social status than the students who lived in apartments, it seemed. I was a neglected child, but I felt like I was more at home socially than the well-cared for children that lived in apartments. And these apartments in particular were closer to Cheltenham School District so it was as though you weren't even considered a proper Abington student, at least socially. But I digress.

I knew this going into it, but I thought, "well, at least we live in Abington Township." He no longer has to lie about where he lives. He had a loving and caring mom at home. He had a nice, clean, and orderly home. He had home-cooked meals and snacks available at all times. I thought at least he doesn't have to worry about those things like I always did. That's when I learned that kids don't necessarily appreciate the finer things or even the bare necessities given to them. They just think, "well, yeah...this is what life is." Children don't typically realize the sacrifices their parents make until they have children of their own. The opposite is also true. When a parent works hard to raise and care for their children, they soon recognize the inadequacies in parenting that they received. This was the case with me. It was really challenging for me to raise my son on my own. And not just on my own, but with people constantly undermining my authority and feeling disrespected by other family members, countering all of my rules and standards.

As difficult as it was, I absolutely loved being a mom, so much so that I totally neglected my own needs. Come to think of it, I was taught to neglect myself, anyway. While raising my son I remember that the altruism and self-sacrifice hurt at times, but I just numbed that part of me and took pride in taking care of him. I loved caring for him. It gave me purpose to provide him with a nice home and to cook his meals, take him to his activities, and make sure he was healthy. My most favorite part was watching him perform. I would think to myself, "I made that?" It caused me to question how a parent, especially a mother, would not want to raise her children? It can be so rewarding.

Parenting is generally instinctual in my opinion and emotionally rewarding no matter how bad it appears to turn out in the end. You hope that the hard times don't last long. You hope to see a healthy return on your investment. Proverbs 22:6 states, "Train up a child in the way he should go: and when he is old, he will not depart from it" (*KJV*). This is a promise. If you bring them up in the nurture and admonition of the Lord (Ephesians 6:4, *KJV*), you should be okay in the end. For a long time, we prayed together and we went to church just about every Sunday.

Because of the distance we lived from school, my son was considered "a walker". However, we lived in the grey zone where we were too far to walk to school but not quite two miles away to qualify to take the bus. It was a bit too far to walk, in my opinion. I somehow managed to get the bus route from the school for the "bussers" closest to the apartments. My son and I did a dry run twice before the first day of school, where I walked with him to the bus stop. Other kids in the apartments took the same school bus so he had people with whom he could walk to and from the bus stop with. I worked in the Olde City section of Philadelphia at the time. To commute to work I would either walk down the driveway to the *Regional Rail* or drive to *Fern Rock* station and get on the *Broad Street Line* to the *Market-Frankford El*. Life was pretty good that year, without too many ups and downs.

Matthew then started getting into a lot of fights at school. He began getting suspended. Though I had my issues growing up, I was unfamiliar with this level of trouble. My siblings and I never got suspended that I know of. One time I was about to get suspended and I started balling in the principal's office. I guess the principal knew that I would be safer in school. For Matthew, the problems started at McKinley and they just kept escalating. But we all know that it first starts in the home. However, the behavioral problems at school were all so foreign to me. My siblings and I just didn't get into this much trouble. Not that we were perfect but we were too afraid to let our parents find out anything we did.

I was mischievous as a kid, but I wasn't considered bad. My parents came to the school a couple of times but it was mainly because of my grades. My dad came up just because he was interested and always involved in my schooling. Growing up, however, I don't recall me, my brother, or my sister having any serious delinquent behavior.

Though I sometimes drank alcohol just for the fun of it and to lower my inhibitions, I never got caught. While I didn't give my parents as much trouble as Matthew gave me, I realize that the apple doesn't fall too far from the tree. From what she tells me, my mother also got into trouble in school. However, where my son's behavior at school was concerned, me having to get involved at such an intense level was foreign territory for me. Although I was able to, it was nearly impossible for me to hold down a job; I had to be at his school so much. However, I made sure I was present and answered the call of duty, continuing to rise to the occasion whenever necessary.

Keep in mind, that I am a petite, very young-looking Black woman. Not a good combination where Black boys are concerned, especially in suburban America. Stereotypically I was not adequately respected by the staff even though I was somewhat a product of the township. In fact, I'd probably been there longer than some of the staff. I was really thankful however, that the principal at McKinley (until his last year) was a Black woman and his principals at Abington Junior and Senior High were also Black. They at least listened to me and gave me some respect because of my involvement and concern for my son's education.

After all, I carried myself well, was educated and was well-spoken. I was very involved in my son's life (education, extra-curricular activities, etc.). We were not on Section 8 or any other type of assistance. I worked, at this point, sometimes two jobs. You could tell my son was well cared for. Regardless, he continued to act out at home, school, and in the community. Initially, I was sympathetic to him and on his side, but after a while I simply could not dismiss the part he played in each situation.

My best-friend (at the time) and I travelled to the Bahamas when we graduated from college. Therefore, I wanted to take Matthew to an island similar to that. Since I had never been to Jamaica, I wanted to take him there. I knew he would love the natural scenery and all-inclusive resort experience so the summer before Matthew went into the eighth grade, he and I travelled to Jamaica with some cousins. I had hoped that once he saw how privileged we are as Americans and realized how we lived compared to those in other countries, it might influence his behavior for the better. While he indeed loved snorkeling, he didn't fully appreciate the trip the way I'd hoped he would. I really thought he'd appreciate the contrast in the quality of life between the two countries.

Throughout his life I tried very hard to socialize him because I knew that being an only child wouldn't always be easy. He went to quality day camps and overnight camps. His calendar was packed with almost every activity you can imagine. At times I felt like I was nothing more than a taxi service. He was in *Y-Achievers*, and *Y- Leaders* with the *YMCA*, church activities, soccer, karate, boxing, basketball, separate academic and reading tutors, taekwondo, baseball, acting, preventative counseling. You name it! I put him in extra reading classes just because I wanted him to be a good reader. While I was driving to my grandmother's in the morning so he could go to McKinley, I used to make him read to me. That was music to my ears.

Proactively, I got him a therapist because growing up, I never had anyone to talk to. I wanted to make sure that if he felt he couldn't talk to me, at least he'd have someone unbiased to share his thoughts with. I tried really hard not to repeat any unhealthy cycles. He started guitar lessons in the sixth grade and he was really good at it. He glowed when he played but eventually the novelty and my momentum wore out for him. Additionally, I did not have the funds for him to continue with a private guitar teacher. You could see in his eyes how much he loved guitar and boxing. He also had a *Big Brother* in elementary school whom he loved. I tried to get him a Big Brother again while he was in junior high but for some reason it just didn't work out. I don't remember why now but I think it had something to do with a waiting list. Some people believe that I may have overcompensated. I probably did. Goulston and Goldberg (1996) suggest in their book, *Get Out of Your Own Way*, that when someone is neglected, they sometimes over-compensate for their children, which can come off as controlling to the child. My son would probably say that's true. I was simply trying to be the mother I didn't have. I recognized some deficits in his self-image and I didn't want him to fall through the cracks.

I found a Police Athletic League (PAL) program in our neighborhood that he liked, but he got in trouble there; throwing candy and vandalizing the library. He had to go before a group of sponsors to determine if he would be allowed to continue. I don't remember what the outcome was, however, that soon fizzled out. I also signed him up for the *Kappa Achievement Academy*, a mentorship program sponsored by the *Kappa Alpha Psi Fraternity*. His paternal uncle had mentioned it to me. He participated for about a year. One weekend in the summer he went away to *Temple University*, Ambler Campus for one of their retreats but got into a fight and was not welcome back. I was really at a loss. What was brewing under the surface at that time?

His bad behavior continued during seventh and eighth grade. We'd gone to church pretty much every Sunday, from the time he was four. We consulted with pastors to no avail until we started going to a specific church. I even had a pastor from our church in Ardmore come up and advocate for us when I tried to get him into *Valley Forge Military Academy*. I was so grateful to have a man present, willing to advocate for me. He was an elderly man but at least I wasn't alone in trying to advocate for my son. Matthew, later told me that he failed the entrance exam on purpose. I also began the process for him to attend Milton Hershey School. I took his dad to court for sole custody and he didn't fight it. I needed to do this in order for him to qualify to attend Hershey. Meanwhile, my older brother, sister, and others interfered with my plans for him by telling him he didn't need to go there and offering him that he could stay with them. No one respected my position as his mother and people constantly infringed upon my rights to raise him the way I'd hoped. My brother told him he could live with him, though he could barely take care of himself and had a daughter of his own that he wasn't raising.

My brother's interference came as a surprise to me because we never had a problematic relationship. It was just a common theme throughout my family to undermine my role as Matthew's mother. There was no one I could turn to. No one, it seemed, respected the fact that if I had a child, no matter the circumstances, I was going to raise my child, through hell or high water. I felt like I was fighting a strong force to keep my child in my care. I was determined not to let anyone from my dysfunctional family raise my child.

People suggested that I was always trying to send him away but I was simply trying to protect him from me and my family. It seemed no one trusted my judgment. I am and have always been intelligent. I knew what I was doing. I trusted me. However, because of the pushback and constant interference from many, there was a lot of conflict in my home. I tried to be strong and move forward not only for me but so that I could be there for Matthew. We all know how important a father is to a family, but through my observations I have learned that boys need a strong my mom in their life as well.

Through the church we belonged to I tried to get him into *Boy Scouts*. At the initial meeting he acted out so badly, using profanity, and protesting about enrolling that I was embarrassed. However, I remember the young men formed a circle around him one day after church and prayed for him. I remember seeing a change for about a day. One of the young men reached out to me and volunteered to mentor him, which he did for about a year. That soon fizzled out.

I wrote to Dr. Phil, Greg Mathis, Steve Harvey, and Oprah Winfrey to no avail. I considered taking him to the *Scared Straight* program right before he entered the ninth grade but we would've had to go up to

Rahway prison and neither I nor he felt ready for that. I felt the same way when a social worker suggested I sign him up for boot camp. I'd read stories about what happens to some kids who attend such camps and I didn't want to subject him to that just yet. He was still my "special little guy." I still saw him as my baby.

I took him to an academic tutor because I just wanted to give him a leg up in the classroom. They had to test him first to see what level he was on. I believe they administered the *Kaufman Test of Education Achievement.* When the results came in, the facilitator came out to discuss his results with me and said, "he scored extremely high in every category and this is a very reputable test...I don't really understand what he's doing here." I then started to concentrate more on his social development. Nothing seemed to be effective however.

I believe it was the spring of his eighth-grade year that he and his friends did something really bad and consequently got into significant trouble. When the cops called me to pick him up from the police station, I replied: "no, he's not coming back here, you keep him." Sometimes we have to face the fact that even though we are their parent and would like to raise them at home, it just might not be the best place for the child at that time. We also need to face the fact that there are times when problematic behavior becomes so significant that another environment may be necessary.

During this tumultuous time, I confided a lot in my step-mother. She told me she thought he was, "acting like a child who is unloved." I didn't disagree with her. I had raised him purely off of what I'd learned in my early childhood education classes. I had no other blueprint to follow. I never had an opportunity to say: "I'm ready and prepared to have a baby...let me bring a child into this world." I loved my son and no doubt his presence prompted me to take life a little more seriously. Being his mom made me even more determined to finish undergrad, but I was essentially forced to raise him. I still pray for him and myself...and to me, he was still a perfect little boy. He was just beautiful and perfect in every way. One of my cousins once called him "Baby Billy Dee." Sometimes I felt like God made him so beautiful so that I would have no choice but to love him. It remains however, that it's not right for a child to be put in a situation where his mother felt "forced" to raise him. We went to another therapist together and when the therapist later spoke to me in private, he said: "he just wants a mother." That's when I realized that that's essentially all he wanted...and a father.

Although my parents didn't raise me, they were 30 and 42 when I was born, and well able to make the decision whether or not to have me. Either way you look at it, I was wanted. Whether it was because a childless, forty-two-year-old man wanted badly to have child or that this thirty-year-old woman wanted to have a baby in order to keep this man, no matter the reason, I was wanted. That being said, my parents had a level of love for me. I think that initial connection with them is what kept me going. I can honestly say that in my early years I really felt loved. Though I was neglected by my grandmother during the school week, I still felt loved by my mother from the time I was born to the age of 11, and have always felt loved by my dad. They may not have raised me in the traditional sense, but whenever I was around them, I definitely felt loved.

I'm not sure that Matthew ever felt that from either one of his parents and I realize now that it's just not right. I wanted him to have as much love as possible. I can remember times when Matthew tried to bond with me and I rejected him. It was a cycle that was easy for me to understand given I was only 16 when I had him, but how can you explain why my mom did it? Regardless, I was perpetuating a cycle of detachment. This is a pathological illness that occurs when one is basically "sleep walking." In order for generations to stop cycles, someone has to "wake up," so to speak, and be aware of what is going on, then choose to do something differently. I tried to break many other cycles, but I am ashamed that I continued this one in some ways. Most of the time, however I was conscious and aware and trying to do the right thing whether I felt like it or not. And truth be told, I made a tremendous number of sacrifices to ensure Matthew had everything he needed available to him.

Looking back however, during preparations for my senior prom, Matthew was in the hospital with pneumonia and I decided not to pick him up. I was too concerned about getting to my hair appointment then to my prom. I regret that decision and beat myself up about it to this day. I can still see his little face. My mom came to relieve me. I am really embarrassed to write these words but I only did the best I could with the internal resources I had at the time. After all, I was just a child myself. As a result of the dysfunction at home and in his family, it is no wonder he developed all of these behavioral issues. I think I spent most of my life trying to make up for all of the things I'd done wrong in his early years...

I have always loved and cared about him, but at times I was emotionally detached. I also believe this is why our relationship is so strained. He doesn't remember it obviously, but he felt it and perhaps he didn't receive the proper levels of oxytocin in his early years. This is a chemical that develops in a baby during the initial bonding with a caregiver. Proper development helps form healthy attachments and helps the child develop healthy insight growing up. I believe this is also a source of so many of his behavioral issues and possible attachment issues. Children with positive attachment bonds to their caregivers tend to better resist the urge to engage in substance use, have more positive peer relationships, have more social competence, and demonstrate better coping skills than adolescents who've had a more troubled experience with their parents (Doweiko, 2015).

I remember when Matthew was about eight or nine years old. He had asthma and I had no experience with this. I put "Holy Water" on his chest and prayed over him. I said, "no...my son is not dealing with this for the rest of his life," and to my knowledge, he hasn't since. He said he only had one more asthma attack but after that his asthma was gone. He is 29 now and hasn't complained about asthma since. I remember that after I prayed over him, he said, "now I know you love me." That let me know that he really hadn't felt loved by me before. Another heart-breaking event was when he was around seven; he drew a picture of me lying in bed (I can tend to be a bit lazy sometimes), and on the back of the picture he wrote, "I love you; do you love me?" It seems my baby never felt loved by his own mother. I've said, "I'm sorry" to him a million times and I feel that I can't say it enough. I constantly pray for strength for the both of us to eventually overcome this and become whole.

I've always been very open and honest with Matthew about everything because I didn't want him to think he was crazy for feeling a certain way. I instilled in him that his feelings were valid so he would never doubt himself, even when it came to me. I have heard mental health professionals state that a rebellious child is the one who is the most sensitive and who is crying out, trying to tell everybody within and without the family that something is wrong. When I was growing up, we were not encouraged to speak up for ourselves. I for one was to be seen and not heard. However, I constantly encouraged Matthew to speak up for himself.   I may not have been very nurturing, but I was definitely a conscientious parent.

As previously mentioned, my mom got him dressed every morning during his first year of life and took him to the lady's house down the street who watched him. I remember saying goodbye to him one morning while he was still in his crib and him frowning the way babies do. During my first two years of college I stayed on campus, only coming home on weekends. I didn't have a daily presence in his life until he was two, going on three. On top of this, he didn't have a dad to whom he could look up to or emulate. In addition, some of his behavioral traits are genetic. I pray he forgives me and I pray for love and wholeness in both of our lives. I was always happy for the unconditional love his paternal grandmother showed him. I always encouraged it until it began to interfere with the rules in my home, my standards and expectations for him.

There were a lot of people who showed my son love. And I never got in the way of it because I wanted him to have as much support as possible. His paternal grandmother's love was 100% unconditional and for that, I'm grateful. I'd wanted him to experience that kind of love because I hadn't. He is blessed to have had her in his life. He actually had three grandparents who loved him. Overall, he had a good grandparent experience. My son will always have me but I never want to get in the way of him receiving as much healthy love as possible.

I was just going through the motions with Matthew. I had to do the act of loving him until I felt the deep feelings. I instinctually loved him from the time I saw him but I don't think it was the real love that a mother is supposed to feel for her child. It's really sad when I think about it. I deserve to feel unconditional love for Matthew and he deserves the feeling a child should have for his mother. It appears however that Matthew really still doesn't get the concept that I'm his mother.

I asked one of my dearest friends why she thought I was having so many problems with him. She said, "it's because you went away to school for those first two years of his life." She went on to ask, "does Matthew see you as his mother or does he see you as a person that he loves?" I thought, "That's it!" Matthew would say that he sees me as his mother (because he doesn't know any better), but deep down, I think he just sees me as a lady that took care of him; that he loves. Sometimes I think I may be the cause. Maybe, because I was so young when I had him that I gave off a youthful energy. I hope he will learn to recognize me as his mother, but I know that will take effort on his end and continued maturation in both of us. Now that he is almost 30, we both have to be conscientious about rebuilding our relationship as mother and son. Part of it is my fault due to the emotional distance and the immaturity as it pertains to motherhood. And much of it is due to generational implications. Emotionally, I've always been a little immature in some ways, primarily because adults didn't really talk to me, growing up. No one had any sort of stimulating conversation with me and I was not encouraged to express myself. One thing for sure, I may not have had to capacity to bond with Matthew the way I wished I could, but I definitely adored him and made sure he had everything he needed. He and I were a little family especially when we lived away from family interference.

Because I am the youngest (I wasn't raised with my siblings on my dad's side), for the longest time I really was my mom's "baby." When I was with her, I wasn't really held accountable for anything, probably because she only saw me on weekends during the school year and for two months each summer. When I was with her, other than doing the dishes, I didn't have any real responsibilities growing up. Everything was done for me. I began to feel really uncomfortable with this as I got older. I fought it when I was around 19, at which time I wanted to be more independent and take responsibility for raising my son. I wanted to grow into my own person which was difficult because I also wanted to do right by my child and grow into the mother role, full-time. She tried so hard to keep me dependent on her. It was difficult to navigate all of this simultaneously but I did.

Between the ages of 14 to 17 my son alternated between alternative schools and group homes. They actually made me pay room and board for him to be in those placements. I really wanted him to be there during the summer because otherwise, he would go down to North Philly and I knew he was already unhinged. And him spending idle time down there would have been a disaster. With much prayer he survived and is still here and free to this day. It was at that time that I realized God had entrusted him to me to raise. I had to work hard, not only to do right by Matthew, but to do right by God who loves him more than anyone can.

Chapter 7

Navigating Interference

When my family first found out that I was pregnant at 16, my cousin offered to raise my child. My older sister offered to take my son as well. Knowing how my family was, I knew that would absolutely have been the wrong move. I knew it was a setup and knew that eventually they would speak of me as some failure who had a child yet didn't raise him. My child was not going to be bounced around from family member to family member like I had been. I knew better.

To this day, some of my family members insist that I didn't raise him and insinuate that I wasn't really there for him, even though the evidence speaks to the contrary. This is called cognitive dissonance, which means you believe what you want to believe even in the face of evidence proving otherwise. I think people use cognitive dissonance because, in some way it helps them survive and justify their opinions. It helps them deal with their perceptions of their own inadequacies I suppose.

I may not have been the best mother but I did the best I could with what I had at the time. Would Matthew's outcome have been different if another family member had raised him? We will never know but he is my son and it is my job to take care of him.

Ironically, neither one of my parents really know me. While growing up and into my 20's and 30's, people could pretty much tell them anything about me and they had no idea if it was true or not. I never wanted that to be the case for me and any of my kids (if I had more). No one can tell me anything about Matthew that I don't already know. I know him through and through. I will admit that as an adult I probably don't know him as much as I did when he was growing up but I know his core. After all, I raised him. Living with someone and going on vacations (even if just for a few days), is the best way to get to know someone. Which is a good thing to keep in mind when dating. I can honestly say that the only people who really know me are Matthew and my older brother because they are the only people I've ever lived with for any significant length of time. I know them probably better or just as much as anyone else.

If someone else in my family would've raised him, it would've been weird to be around him while acting like we were "cousins" or "aunt/nephew" or whatever, when in fact we are mother and son. I recognize that this happens in families and that there is nothing wrong with it...to each his own. As for me, that would simply have been too weird. I wasn't having that in my life. I want transparency...good, bad, or indifferent (or as my good girlfriend once said – or beautiful). No matter how it appears to others, I was essentially born into all this dysfunction, which I didn't create, and I've tried to navigate it as best I could.

We went through so much during this time. Matthew had begun to speak disrespectfully to me. I can't remember what it was he said at the time but one day, I grabbed a frying pan and scared him with it. I had never seen anyone do this. I had talked to someone who told me their mother acted as if she was going to hit him with a frying pan so I just did the same to my son just to scare him. He had the nerve to call the cops on me. When they arrived, they chewed him out telling him, "if you talked to my wife life that I'd knock your teeth out." Matthew later told me that his paternal grandmother told him that if he ever felt scared, he should call the cops on me. Seriously? He ran away once and I couldn't find him for a couple of hours so I called the cops. They found him at a sneaker store and he came back home. I don't remember if they brought him home or if they met him at the apartment. Either way, both he and the cops ended up at the apartment together and they told him to "just do what your mother tells you to do."

Another time he was sitting at the table doing his homework and kept making careless errors. I kept telling him to correct an item and he ripped the paper up and said, "I'm sick of this shit!" I believe I actually "put him out" (in the vestibule of the apartment) after his outburst. I put his sneakers in the vestibule with him and told him to call his grandmother. I called the cops and told on myself. They told me how wrong I was and looking back now, that was not the right thing to do, but I was at my wits end with him and his disrespect towards me. Previously, after some infraction, I'd taken him to his father's house for a talking to, but his father beat him so I knew I could never take him over there ever again.

I never really had him around his dad much though I didn't stop him from seeing him if he wanted to. Matthew never really expressed interest in seeing his dad. However, while we were in a counseling session, the therapist asked him about his dad and Matthew, on the verge of tears, said, "he doesn't want me." That broke my heart. I didn't know he felt that way until that moment. His dad knew him because there were times when Matthew's paternal grandmother got them together.

Anyway, this newfound rebellion was something I was completely unfamiliar with. I'd never had interactions with the cops in my life. No cops had ever been to my home growing up---ever! I didn't know the first thing about calling the cops on someone. I didn't know this until he called the cops on me after having been given instruction to do so. When they came and sided with me, I thought, "finally, I have some support...maybe they can help me with his behavior because my family certainly wasn't."

As mentioned previously, he and his paternal grandmother were extremely close. However, I remember having to tell her on multiple occasions to stop interfering. I had to remind her that this was my child and that I would ask for help if I needed it. She didn't listen and it got to the point that they were in cahoots against me. Recall that we lived quite far from his school. I discovered that when he was around 15 years old and attending Abington Senior High, his grandmother would meet him at the corner of our apartment complex and drive him to school without my knowledge. Initially, I'd advocated for him to be able to take the bus. I'd spoken to the authorities at the school to get approval because they'd put the kibosh on kids from our apartment complex taking the bus. I knew it was a good distance from there to the school but at that point, I wanted him to walk, simply because there were no other options. I couldn't drive him every day. I thought to myself that maybe this would help him build character. Either way, no one should have been picking him up without my permission and surely, had they asked me if it was ok, I would've agreed to it. Why all the secrecy? It only served to undermine my authority.

During a meeting with a detective from the Police Athletic League, I explained that he was confused partially because my authority was constantly being undermined. The mediator then told his paternal grandmother that if she didn't stop interfering, the only one who would suffer was him. Another time, Matthew and I were in a counseling session when her name came up again. The therapist asked me if his grandmother might join us for a session and when she agreed, he suggested she seek counseling as to why she was continuously interfering. She never changed her behavior and it was as if everything we'd discussed went right over her head.

Matthew's grandmother lived two townships away in Hatboro-Horsham Township, whereas we lived in Abington Township. She then sold her home in Horsham and bought one in Willow Grove, right in Abington Township. I found out later that she then picked my son up at the corner, without my permission to take him to "see his room." I never understood the need for all the secrecy.

Nonetheless, when he was about 15 years old, he started staying at her place more often. She essentially lived three to four miles down the road from our apartment so he remained enrolled in the same school district. As was his tendency at the time, he ended up getting in trouble again and was sent away to a youth facility then to a group home. In a strange twist of fate, I ended up having to pay tuition and room and board for him simply so he could attend these alternative schools. Remember, we didn't have any government assistance.

When Matthew was around 12, his dentist recommended braces. I thought it was too early because all of his adult teeth hadn't come in yet. When I was younger, I had a slight over-bite and a gap in my two front teeth so I thought to myself, "I'm not getting him braces yet…I had teeth just like that and my teeth grew in just about perfectly." Then, one day his grandmother took him to the orthodontist and had them put braces on him without my knowledge, leaving me with a $4,000 bill. She made the initial payment of approximately $300 only because she had to. I, on the other hand, had to pay the balance which I was not prepared to do, though I made the payments every month. After all that, when he was around 14, he decided to use pliers to remove the braces himself. I guess he thought that having braces did not suit his image. I did take him to the orthodontist to get a retainer, but I don't believe he completed that phase.

Around the same time, I'd had enough of the conspiring against me so I went over to his grandmother's house and raised hell. I put on my monkey suit, as my dad would call it, and yelled at the top of my lungs, telling her to, "give me my son back!" I even insinuated that she must have a "sexual stronghold on him," purposefully yelling it to embarrass her. I had had enough! The sad part about it was that she was literally on the phone with my mom at the time. Turns out my mom was actually on her side. I overheard her say to my mom, "she IS sick!" That's how I knew that she was talking to my mom because my mom often said I was "sick" and "disturbed." Obviously, I wasn't but I later learned this was her way of projecting. I strongly believe that she just wanted to keep insinuating that I was disturbed to try and justify any circumstantial, inevitable, and unforeseen happenings, in which my name was "dragged up" so she could say, "I told you so."

She never gave me advice, support, or compassion where my son's behavior was concerned. For the sake of the benefit of the doubt, I want to think that maybe she simply didn't know any better. These days however, I rarely give people the benefit of the doubt. Dr. Phil talks about withholding the benefit of the doubt from people in his book *Life Code (2012)*. He speaks on us wanting to think the best of people, though unfortunately, most of the time they know exactly what they're doing. For the most part, insignificance was projected onto me instead of value. It's all just so unfortunate. Again, I pray for healing and wholeness for all involved.

For a long time, when I was a child, I had zero patience for people. If I felt the least bit wronged by someone, I would simply go up to them and punch them in the face. No one ever hit me back. I guess my lashing out came as a surprise because for the most part, I was friendly and personable. My mom had begun to hit me for no reason from the time I was 11 until I was 19. One day she grabbed me by my neck and smacked me because my nephew had fallen down the steps. I had absolutely nothing to do with it as I was in the kitchen at the time. I'd had enough and smacked her back, yelling, "stop hitting me!" I now regret this along with all of my adverse behavior, but where this instance is concerned, I was just so sick of her hitting me for no reason. I never considered myself an angry person, though to some degree, I suppose I was. Deep down, I think my mom takes a certain amount of pleasure in knowing about the strain I experience in the relationship between my son and me.

Though I got into some fights while in school, I never considered myself a "fighter." I suppose however that I was angry, impatient, and very short tempered, which is such a stark contrast from who I am today. When I look back at the person I was in high school and prior, I don't even recognize myself. Back then, I thought I was invincible. I was so lost and rightfully so. The neglect, dysfunction, and abuse were debilitating. I read somewhere that it is true growth when you look back and don't recognize the person you once were, and can acknowledge the negative behavior that once existed.

My mom kept fueling the fire by telling my son's paternal grandmother that he needed to live with her full time. I realized that my mom was jealous because I was raising my child in a completely different way from the way she chose *not* to raise me. How dare Karima outdo her? I was extremely low on the totem pole in our family in her eyes. I've also heard that many women are jealous of their daughters. It's strange. I can't fathom why you might be jealous of your own child. After discovering that my mother had suggested my son live with his grandmother instead of with me, my heart literally felt like it had been ripped out of my chest. I remember going over to my friends' house that night in tears.

My son's grandmother passed away in the fall of 2018 and Matthew took it especially hard. His grieving process was severe. I don't know if he will ever really get over it. Today, he and I talk openly about everything, including the situation with his grandmother. He believes that she didn't mean to interfere. He says she was just doing what she thought was right. He believes that she saved his life. I now understand why he feels this way and his feelings are valid. I really believe that my mom was jealous that I chose to raise my son and wanted to do anything in her power to sabotage my efforts.

In some strange way, she wanted to sort of cast me aside, but didn't want any other woman to develop a loving relationship with me. Initially, Ann (Matthew's grandmother) and I really liked each other. I thought she was one of the sweetest people on earth. She showed me how to decorate and install curtains. She was the DIY queen. She had Matthew make me Mother's Day collages and other creative gifts.

Matthew loved his grandmother and I am grateful for that. If he felt he wasn't receiving pure love from anyone else, he definitely felt it from her. Everyone deserves to have that special kind of bond that comes only from the relationship between a grandparent and their grandchild. And he had it. I would also add that I know he received pure love from my dad too. Additionally, my mom basically raised him for the first two and a half years of his life and I really think he bonded with her. He had the ideal grandparent experience, in a sense; something I didn't have. I was always grateful for that.

Chapter 8

A Challenging Teenager

I believe he violated his probation which is why at 16, he had to go to another group home. I remained involved in his life and came up for parent's day to visit him. No matter what and no matter where he was, from pre-k through high school, I've always been involved in his education and always been known to the staff as an engaged parent.

While at that home, he met another troubled teen. When he was eventually granted permission to come home on weekends, I had plenty of condoms waiting for him that I'd gotten for free at *Planned Parenthood.* I knew he was around that age and I did not want him to have any excuses for getting anyone pregnant. I started to picture a little girl on Matthew's wall, and then I saw pictures of another little girl, holding a baby. I already knew what was coming.

From the time he was around 11, I continuously had to ask myself, "what's next?" I couldn't believe how much his behavior had gotten progressively worse. It was almost as if he would ask himself: "hmmm...what deviant behavior can I tackle that I haven't already engaged in?"

Sometime in November of 2008 Matthew told me he was indeed going to have a baby. I thought, "alright...I've had enough!" There was nothing else I could do. My child was the boy, not the girl. I made plans to get out of dodge. I worked really hard for him not to repeat any cycles. I raised him. I wasn't raised. He was cared for. I wasn't cared for. He was attended to. I wasn't attended to. I talked to him. No one talked to me. Even if he felt he couldn't talk to me, I put a therapist and so many other mentors in place so that he could at least talk to someone.

Nobody did that for me. I had been a mother since I was 16 years old. I had such high hopes for my life; and his, actually. I wanted to be a TV anchor or perform in musicals. I wanted to pledge in a sorority. I chose not to do any of those things because I chose to be fully present for my child. I invested a lot of time, money, energy, blood, sweat, and tears into him. I used to go into the bathroom at work and sob for hours about my son while I witnessed him self-destruct, and there was nothing I could do but watch it happen. What a horrible feeling.

Upon hearing of the possibility of him having a baby, I decided I was not going to raise another child that I did not willingly choose to bring into this world. It was as if, throughout my life, I hadn't mattered. I felt completely disregarded. And now, even my son was feeling that way towards me. I believe this was partially because I taught him that he mattered more than anyone, and partially because he'd constantly witnessed me being disregarded and disrespected by my family. I felt as if he thought, "I don't care about how she feels, she's just going to have to help." Regardless of the reasoning or what anyone thought...I was out. I wasn't about to stay around and put up with such an outcome after I had done everything in my power for him not to continue along a destructive path. Sometimes I wish I'd had more kids so he wouldn't have been an only child. I believe he may have decided to have a child of his own because he was lonely.

My first experience as a mother was so traumatic for me and him, therefore, I was determined not to have another child unless I was married. That was the closest thing to a guarantee that a man would stay ensuring I wouldn't have to go through single motherhood again. Because my dad was not always around, it was subconsciously ingrained in my head that men don't stay. However, he also taught me that one should be involved in their children's education and fight for them when necessary. Of course, I know now that some men do stay under the right circumstances, but I would never again willingly put a child in a single-parent situation.

Much of the suffering and pain my son and I went through was all so unnecessary. However, Viktor Frankl posits that we should find meaning in the suffering. That is the key. Nonetheless, I had done my best with him and had certainly cared for him in a way that I was not cared for. In any case, I just couldn't take his behavior anymore. I left four months before his 18th birthday. At that point I knew he was not going to change any time soon. I believe that leaving at that time in his life was the right thing to do for him and for me and I have not regretted it.

Chapter 9

Generational Curses

Families have unspoken codes of behavior, expectations, and a certain image they would like to project in society. However, some unspoken ways of behaving and functioning can become pathological and unhealthy. When one is not aware of these patterns or of what is truly going on under the surface, it is very easy to subconsciously pass them down to the next generation.

Marilyn Hickey gives a great sermon on breaking generational curses. If you believe the Bible you can attest to the veracity of curses present therein. The Old Testament notes many instances of curses, while the New Testament eases our minds with the assertion that Jesus took all the curses on the cross, thus paying for any Old Testament curses. Christ has redeemed us from the curse of the law, being made a curse; for it is written; cursed is everyone that hangeth on a tree (Galatians 3:13, *KJV*). I think I would be remiss in telling my story without some mention of family curses and how this concept plays out in my life.

Exodus 20:5 states that the sins of the father are visited upon the fourth generation. The scripture specifies that this is true for those that hate God. In fact, every man will answer for his own sins but the *weakness to sin* will come down to four generations. What does this mean for me? No, my parents were not perfect; no one is. But I don't have to pay for their sins. They will have to pay for their own.

However, since they did not raise me up in the nurture and admonition of the Lord, and because they neglected my most basic developmental needs while trying to get their own needs met, a curse was passed down to me. I in turn passed that curse down to Matthew. I called myself putting Matthew's needs before my own, leaving him with a primary caregiver who lacked many of the necessary internal resources to effectively nurture him. I later identified the *weakness to sin* that was passed down was that of feeling unloved, causing us to look for love "in all the wrong places."

My father's mother passed away when he was only 12 years old. It seems my mom was loved by her my dad, though I'm not sure it was the case with her mother. My parents aren't vocal about their past at all (at least not to me). Sometimes, however, you just need to look at the present to understand the past. Notwithstanding, the feeling of being unloved and unwanted was passed down to me.

Matthew's behavior as a teen was an outward display of him feeling unloved. Incidentally, Matthew and I both acted out in such a way that it was evident we were searching for something to fill a void.

Consequently, today I do my best to make sure my grandson Johnathan feels loved and special at all times, and he definitely knows he's loved by his dad. Though based on what I observed early on, the love he receives from his mom has been questionable in the past. Recently however, I've seen a more outward display of affection from his mother toward him and I can tell that he loves my mom. Hopefully that is an indication that he feels loved by her.

Marilyn Hickey references a section in the Bible that indicates that there are evil spirits familiar with families, that reappear in each succeeding generation to tempt in a similar area of weakness. As you read previously, these sin patterns can only be perpetrated onto those who hate the Lord. I take this to mean those who do not put His Word first in everything they do and who do not teach their children to do the same. Though my dad taught me principles like "cleanliness is next to godliness" and "obey your parents." Living according to God's word was not taught to me nor was it demonstrated for me, or even expected of me. I didn't live with them so how could they impart these principles to me?

I, on the other hand, did teach my son God's principles. In Deuteronomy Chapter 6, the Bible states that you are supposed to talk to your kids at home and away, about the word of God and how to apply it to daily living. I did this. My son and I went to church together, prayed together, and I always explained how to apply the word as best I could. And Proverbs Chapter 22 says to "train up a child in the way he should go and when he gets older, he will not depart from it." I remember learning this scripture when he was around 13 and being told that this was a promise. I always kept that in mind, waiting for the day that I would see it manifested.

The actions in regards to demonstrating my love for God are heretofore. Incidentally, the good news is that the Bible goes on to teach us that for those that love God, He will bless them to the thousandth generation. Therefore, me and my next generations should not be cursed. We should be blessed. It only takes one person to break a curse. For example, my dad has said that his dad was an alcoholic. My dad never let his children see him drink alcohol and I'm not sure if he even drank it at all. Therefore, none of his kids or grandkids have that affliction. Perhaps the enemy was trying to tempt me in this area as a teen. I did not like the taste of it and I had too many other pro-social interests that meant more to me. Drinking alcohol just did not hold my interest as much as social and performance endeavors for the most part.

My son, however, got a double dose. His father is an alcoholic, and his great-grandfather is one also. I'm not sure about my son's paternal grandfather. As many teenagers do; my son experimented with drugs and alcohol. This was the enemy reappearing throughout succeeding generations in more ways than one. It will surely try to attack Johnathan. Therefore, we will have to be mindful and have open communication with him so he can identify the attacks, recognize what's going on, and respond with: "no enemy, you are not going to get me!"

Some behaviorists contend that teens literally experience something akin to psychosis, a chemical imbalance if you will. The chemicals in the brain are unstable during that transition period from childhood to adulthood, which is a large part of why they sometimes make poor choices and bad decisions.

We must encourage our teenagers to find positive hobbies and activities they are interested in to keep them busy and engaged. If possible, it's also good for them to be involved in family activities so they feel that they fit into a group. At the very least, they should be heavily supervised, otherwise they might end up making decisions that could ruin their lives. In fact, as I've told Matthew, many teens don't even make it out alive. To those reading this, you're still here for a reason: there's a purpose for your life.

Also, as it relates to the enemy going from generation to generation, these patterns are not only spiritual, they are also physical. Doctors know this which is why when you fill out your intake paperwork you have to indicate your medical history. They want you to document any ailments that have affected your parents and or grandparents because the doctors believe that you may have the same. The enemy tried to attack my son with asthma. I prayed over him. It came back the next generation to try to enter my grandson. I prayed over him as well. I haven't heard of any asthma attacks from either one of them in recent years. However, I will keep it in the back of my mind so that I can bind the enemy if I see it resurface.

Ironically, generational curses affected my family in another way; my mom wanted to be a dancer (as did I). She had her heart set on it. For some reason, her father wouldn't allow her to continue. As I was growing up, I always told her that I wanted to be an actress. She would respond with: "get in the real world." She never supported me. I used to love this movie called *Really Rosie*. I remember Really Rosie had a director's chair. I saw a director's chair in a magazine and asked my mom to get it for me. She looked at me with seething disapproval asking, "why do you want that?" My dreams were crushed. In as much as my mom's dreams were crushed by her my dad, she then turned around and tried to crush mine. Another example of negative inter-generational behavior.

Marilyn Hickey explains how the attacks get worse from generation to generation. Matthew 12:43-45 states: "when the unclean spirit is gone out of a man, he walketh through dry places seeking rest and findeth none," then he says, "I will return into my house from whence I came out. And when he comes, he finds it empty, swept, and garnished; then goeth he and taketh with himself seven other spirits more wicked than himself. And they enter in and dwell there and the last state of that man is worse than the first." She purports that what they mean by "house" is generation. What this means is that when you become a born-again believer and start to break cycles or generational curses the enemy has to leave. But he is going to go out and get seven worse than himself to tempt the next generation, not just seven times that of the previous generation but to a worse degree or extent than the previous one.

So how do you break a curse? Matthew 17:21 says this comes about by prayer and fasting. Praying and fasting applies when you see your children going off track. Take action. Get up and move your family away if you can. Initiate open and honest communications, no matter how cringeworthy. Teach the younger generations about generational curses and how to watch out for known curses; alcoholism, addiction, anger, poverty, disease, disaster. Finally, I would say that we have to learn the biblical and universal laws and principles and act on them, applying them to our lives.

Chapter 10

A New Beginning

Starting in December of 2008, I began submitting my CV to any place in Orlando or Tampa that conducted clinical trials. I was planning to move to Florida when Matthew was eight or nine, however, he began to protest, telling his grandmother that he didn't want to go and she told me, "he can live with me." I was not going to have anyone else raise my son so I stayed as long as I could. Would things have turned out better if I'd let another family member raise him? Or better yet, If I'd taken him with me to Florida anyway? I don't know. Not to mention, out of the two people saying, "he can live with me;" one hadn't raised their own and the other didn't raise a decent person.

Another suggested Matthew would have done better had she raised him, however, she called him stupid once, looking him dead in the eyes, because he'd said it was stupid that they (the child and his mother) were running late to drop him off at school. The adults in Matthew's life were all dysfunctional. You might consider me dysfunctional but I was doing my best to do the right thing when those same elders insisted in negatively interfering. I didn't have any support. I felt I was as much of a victim as he was. Ultimately, however, you cannot play victim. You must use your power to turn everything around to work for your good.

I flew to Tampa twice to interview, once for the University of South Florida and another time at a urologist's office in St. Petersburg. I met my sister at International Plaza and Bay Street and we had dinner at the Blue Martini. At that time Tampa was still "jumpin," and I remember seeing some celebrities that night.

During the summer of 2008 my boyfriend, at the time, and I went down to Florida to visit. We looked at houses together, in a place called New Tampa. It was pretty rural. A second time I went down with my sister and also looked at apartments in New Tampa. I remembered a specific apartment complex and I used the address on all of my CVs. I felt that if I was local, I'd have a better chance of getting an interview. Vetting was much different then...

One day in February of 2009 I was sitting in my car at the Burger King down the street from my apartment in Glenside, using their WiFi. I remember it was snowing, sleeting and cold. I had sent my CV to the *H. Lee Moffitt Cancer Center*. I really had no idea what this place was but they were advertising a clinical research opening on "*Monster.com*." I had only worked on one oncology trial once and had been clueless. Nevertheless, I submitted my CV and got a call a few days later. Keep in mind, the address on my CV was that random apartment complex in New Tampa, but here I was sitting in my cold car in Glenside, PA. On a Thursday in early March, Moffitt called and asked if I could come in for an interview on Monday, March 9, 2009. I promptly stated, "yes, I can be there."

My dad recruited some of my cousins to help me move, taking some of my furniture off my hands. Matthew was staying between my house and his grandmother's at that point. He came and got his stuff that evening. He didn't have much and had pretty much moved out and into his room in a single-family home with his grandmother in Willow Grove. They wanted to be together. I had no more fight left in me.

Although, at times he indicated that he wanted to go with me, I could not go through anymore toxicity with him. By then he was four months shy of turning 18 and was in the 11th grade because he had failed a grade, without the option to attend summer school. He had a child on the way and if I'm not mistaken, he was still on probation. One of the county representatives and others were trying to persuade me take him with me. I told them, under no uncertain terms, was he going with me. After speaking with me several times, though they knew me to be an articulate, educated, hard-working my mom, they refused to respect my decision. Thankfully, my pastor, Pastor Thomas, came with me to the last meeting and advocated for me. They finally listened.

I also knew that it would not be wise for me take him with me because Tampa had a lot of gangs and with him coming so late to a new school and being in the rebellious state of mind he was already in, would have been a disaster. I firmly believe his behavior would have gotten worse.

After I packed up my car that Friday, my boyfriend Ellison and I got on the road to Florida. I know I left my son behind, but I had to grow. My whole life could not consist of constantly arguing with him and putting out his fires. Besides, he wanted to stay with his grandmother anyway, and she was more than willing for him to do so.

Right before we left, my dad gave Ellison a hug. Though I'm sorry to say it, I could tell My dad was thankful that I was getting out of what had turned into a toxic situation, for my son and I. I know that's not the way it's supposed to be but that's just how it was. I know it may be hard to understand and it may seem odd but it's the truth. Turns out he was really upset with me for leaving him and still is. Well guess what: I was really upset at the way he had behaved over the past few years.

I didn't meet my grandson, Johnathan, until he was a year old. My son had to figure this part out on his own and endure two-hour commutes in the cold on public transportation to see his baby. His grandmother helped him somewhat but for the most part, he still lived with her but was on his own where his son's care was concerned. He continued to get into trouble and later told me that he'd almost dropped out of high school. When he was about 21 years old, I ended up buying him a car to help with his commute between work and picking up Johnathan. My dad had bought me a car when I was 19 so I bought one for my son as well.

I wasn't there anymore to constantly bail him out of trouble, until an incident when he was 24. Though I'd been away for almost 10 years, I stepped in. Though he complains that I wasn't there for him, he had to wallow in his own misery for a while in order to grow. I was done paying for his mistakes. I was done living in grief day in and day out. I never envisioned my life would turn out that way. It was time for some tough love. He now had to lie in the bed he'd made for himself while I lived a thousand miles away. If he was bent on destroying his life, he was no longer going to take me with him.

I was really thankful that Ellison drove me down to Tampa. He was a good person. We met in 2007 outside a bar in Germantown, called *Champagne's*. I wasn't interested in him at first but he persisted. I gave him my number and we talked. It turned out that we worked right around the corner from each other in North Wales, PA. We both worked in the pharmaceutical industry. We would meet for lunch sometimes. Occasionally it would be just him and I and sometimes my co-worker joined us. I grew to love Ellison but I wasn't in love with him. He taught me how I should be treated as a woman and I will always be grateful to him for that.

Ellison also dabbled in music production and had helped Matthew record some of his music. I remember him telling me, "I think Matthew's going to be successful and I'd like to be a part of that process." I thought, "wow he really sees something in Matthew - Matthew's really going to be a famous rapper?" Matthew really is an extremely talented lyricist and writer. He has what it takes. All that talent...

Ellison was always there for me. He worked a second job, picking people up from the supermarket and driving them home; kind of like *Uber* before there was an Uber. He would then give me a portion of his earnings though I never asked him for any money. He told me, "I can't wait to take Matthew on a college tour like my dad did me." He even talked about paying for his college which made me feel so good to have someone this supportive in my life. I had never dated nor seen a man with this much chivalry. My dad was always nice to me. He took me on "dates" and opened the car door for me, but I never saw him treat my mom that way. Ellison treated me really well and needless to say, it was like a breath of fresh air. He sometimes bought me clothes and I did the same for him if I happened to be out and saw something he might like.

Ellison held me in high regard. I loved him as a person because he treated me like a queen. I deserved it and I was good to him too. I used to pack his lunch every day for work because he liked to take his lunch. I would sew buttons on his shirts or patch up small holes in his pants. I ironed his clothes for work and I cooked for him.

I tried hard to fall in love with Ellison because he was so good to me and he was always there for me. We went to the gym together and of course we went to church together because that was just who I was. If you were with me, you were going to go church. I realized later however, that he was only going to appease me, not because he had a love for the Word. In fact, a week or so after we went to Palm Sunday service, he still had the palm on his rearview mirror and snatched it down in a way that seemed to dismiss its sacred significance.

One day he said, "what did I do to deserve you? I should be banished to all the horrible woman of the world. I'm the enemy." I had no idea why he might think of himself in this way. I didn't think of him like that at all. I knew he was at times an odd duck (as some may consider me), but I didn't think he was that bad. But even before everyone heard Maya Angelou say it, I knew back then that if someone tells you something about themselves, you'd best pay attention. Later the public learned of Maya Angelou's famous quote, "when people show you who they are, believe them."

One day, Matthew was speaking disrespectfully to me. Ellison had had enough and checked him but

Matthew kept going on with his mouth. Ellison hit Matthew on his cheek with the back of his hand. It wasn't hard but Matthew was offended and didn't take kindly to it. I didn't like it either. We were on our way to drop Matthew off at a group home that Sunday. He came home every weekend and each time it came closer to him returning to the group home, he would start to act out. Prior to Ellison coming around it was just me raising Matthew. When Ellison was there, I at least had a buffer. He and Matthew got into a physical altercation when we dropped him off. Though I didn't think it was right, I didn't blame Ellison, because after all, Matthew was disrespecting someone he loved, which in turn, was disrespectful to Ellison. He explained this to me and I understood. At some point, someone had to check him. I was scared however as I thought maybe the authorities would get involved. After all, Matthew had called the police on me once before. Thankfully, they didn't.

Matthew was my son and not Ellison's so I felt like I couldn't stay with him after what had happened. I would feel like I was choosing a man over my child. My mom did that to me and I never wanted to do that to any of my children. What was Ellison to do, however? I think any decent man would have done the same thing. The thing is, he didn't even get the best of Matthew. It seemed Matthew could hold his own. It was just not a good situation. Really, I should have been happy that anyone stuck around me with my child acting like that. That wasn't the first, second, or third time Ellison witnessed him disrespecting me. He'd just reached his breaking point as anyone would. Unfortunately, the incident was perceived as a win for Matthew. Ellison and I saw very little of each other after that, though he was kind enough to move me to Florida.

We arrived at the apartment complex in Tampa one Saturday morning. They typically didn't allow move-ins on weekends but the apartment manager made an exception. I was grateful because my interview was that Monday. Ellison helped me pick out some stuff at Wal-Mart for the apartment. Believe me, I tried to fall in love with him. Also, I was always open and honest with him about how I felt. Older people used to tell me, "just stay with him, you'll learn to love him." Again, I did love him, I just wasn't in love with him and I didn't want to have kids by him. I knew it would be selfish to not love him but just to use him as a step-father for my son and a protector for myself, even though these were needed roles in my life. I just thought it would be wrong to keep him simply for my own selfish needs when there could be someone else out there that would fall in love with him and willfully give him the children he wanted. Sadly, that Sunday Ellison took a plane back to Philly and I never saw him again. We talked on the phone for a while but our communication fizzled out.

I blame myself a lot for what Matthew and I went through but I realize that it's not so much what I did or didn't do that caused us so much grief. Instead, much of it was because there was no man around for him to emulate or to protect me and the household. Also, for most of my son's life, I was at someone else's mercy where he was concerned and I felt I needed to be around just in case they tried to discredit me or take it out on him and I didn't want that to happen. I knew this and didn't want to put myself or my child in this situation but I had no agency over that part of my life. I'm not saying that I would have parted with Matthew but no matter the decision; it would have been mine, therefore not interrupting the vision I saw in my mind's eye, and possibly preventing the conflict and strife that dominated our lives.

Chapter 11

A New Chapter

Literally and figuratively, I was now in a new chapter in my life. It was the first time I was truly an independent person. I desperately wanted to be the person God created me to be, not a manifestation of the dysfunction I was born into. Of course, as any parent would, after about a year or two of being away from my son, I started to second-guess myself as to whether or not I had been a good mother. Then I would come to my senses remembering that I'd poured my whole life into my child and used to pride myself on being a good my mom.

My parenting choices were put to ease a little when I came across *The Science of Getting Rich* by Wallace D. Wattles. In his book, he states that, "the best thing you can do for the whole world is to make the most of yourself." It is a logical and practical way to look at many situations in life. At all times, people are watching you. You can't control everything but you can make the most of yourself. If nothing else, my hope is that I have set out on a journey to make the most of myself so that Matthew and Johnathan have someone to look up to and so I can give some more.

In the beginning of this new chapter in my life, I thought a lot about changing my name. Although, I've yet to change it, I often wonder if I'd had anointed parents, would "Karima" have been the best name for me? Let's be honest, my parents were not living right at the time of my birth. They were doing what seemed right in their eyes, without any real thought of propriety or how their decisions would affect those around them. I love them but this is the simple truth and I do believe that they did the best they could with the internal resources they had. We all do.

Since then, I have searched and searched, and found that Karima Safiya is the most beautiful name combination I have seen. My dad named me. Karima means generous and Safiya means pure. If you are familiar with the process a diamond goes through towards making it pure, I would have to say that name definitely suits me. I have been through it! The Bible tells us that after you go through many trials and tribulations you will be made perfect. By perfect, I believe the Bible means refined and whole.

After getting settled into my apartment, I went on the interview at Moffitt. I spent the week leading up to it as a nervous wreck. I was still receiving unemployment compensation because the contract with my previous employer had just ended in December. I was able to put a security deposit on the Tampa apartment and I had limited income for another three months or so but that was it. Several days later, I still hadn't heard back from Moffitt so I started looking into substitute teaching, but at the time I believe they only made $26 a day. I was scared. I called Moffitt on Friday morning thinking to myself, "what is it with you people, God sent me down here...I packed up my whole life and moved down here with the expectation that this is my job!" I was walking in blind faith as it turns out; I had landed the job without even knowing it...

My soon-to-be manager told me that I'd already been hired and that HR would be calling me. To say I was happy is an understatement. I'd taken a calculated risk moving to Tampa without having a concrete job offer but I felt confident that I would get one. During the previous three years working in clinical research, head-hunters frequently called our office to recruit my colleagues and I so I knew our profession was in high demand.

I started at Moffitt April 6, 2009. I remember feeling happy and free, even though I felt like I was in a foreign land. New Tampa was true to its name. It was a new development and still pretty rural. The new construction was only a few years old. It was once swamp land, and was quiet and peaceful. I had a pretty high-profile position at Moffitt as an Internal Research Monitor. There were just two of us, Rachel McCoy and myself. Rachel was in her late fifties. She is a gentle soul. We couldn't have looked more different and it turns out she'd advocated for me to get the job. Rachel and I got along really well and had a lot in common in terms of our taste in food and in some of our beliefs. She was a psychiatric Registered Nurse and I learned a lot from her. I felt like this part of my movie was definitely ordained by God!

For the most part, I experienced a seamless transition. As monitors, we traveled up and down the East coast, to different research sites that were participating in Moffitt's clinical trials. Unfortunately, I never quite felt like I belonged in that role. I was thankful for the opportunity and knew it was a blessing, but we're talking about oncology research. Whhaattt? Talk about imposter syndrome. I was clueless, but I went with the flow. I learned as I went, and I guess they were patient with me or maybe they really didn't know what was going on either.

In fact, Moffitt had just started in the clinical research industry a year or two before I'd come on board. Initially, I think all of my co-workers thought that maybe I knew what I was doing. I didn't. All I could do was find discrepancies in the trial data in the database and locate missing and outdated regulatory documents and cite them on my report. I couldn't have a discussion about oncology or research beyond that. Yet, I persisted and even began teaching the monitor's role to incoming employees. I did my best but I could not help feeling like a total imposter the entire time.

During my time in clinical research, I became a world traveler, something I'd never envisioned for myself. My jobs from ICON to Moffitt paid for me to travel to places like LaJolla, CA, North Carolina, Miami, Puerto Rico, and more. While working at ICON, I attended Investigator Meetings. These are usually weekend long meetings held by the sponsor (a pharmaceutical company), where everyone participating in the clinical trial attends to hear more about the investigational product. It was an exciting chapter in my life as I was seeing and learning new things.

If you've ever seen the 1993 movie *The Fugitive* where Harrison Ford interrupts the Investigator as he discusses a new product, the Investigator Meetings were just like that. The event was usually held at a five-star hotel that served gourmet meals. Upon my arrival to some Investigator Meetings there would be a greeter waiting for me, holding up a sign with my name on it. I had some really great experiences. I even presented at an Investigator Meeting in Dallas. Still, I felt like an imposter. I was really nervous and it showed.

While in Tampa, I went to work then came home every day. I found a church home almost immediately, Bible-Based Fellowship Church (Bible-Based for short). I also joined a *Meetup* group whose theme was to go to all the clubs in the Tampa area. I wasn't really a club person at that point in my life and was so involved in church that I knew very little about pop culture and trends. I joined this *Meetup*, however, to see the "lay of the land" so to speak. I had fun, but it got old fast. That just wasn't me anymore. I joined the choir at my church and for the most part I traveled for work. I joined a musical theater group at the Tampa Bay Performing Arts Center and also started singing lessons. I found out through training that I really could sing! However, it takes a lot of training, controlling your breathing and other mechanics. Diaphragmatic breathing: as you inhale, expand your abdomen, as you exhale, contract your abdomen (Travis and Ryan, 2004). It's hard work! While with the *Tampa Bay Performing Arts Center*, we had two performances in front of small audiences.

As previously mentioned, I'd been performing since I was a little girl. One of my first memories is as a cute little four-year-old singing "Twinkle, Twinkle, Little Star" at my pre-school talent show. My son comes by his love of performing honestly. I'm proud that he wasn't afraid to follow through with it. He has performed in front of pretty large crowds. My dad had always supported me in my extra-curricular activities; signing me and my younger siblings up for acting classes, modeling, and gymnastics. He always came to, and recorded my performances at school.

When I was 14, My dad gave a demo tape that my sisters and I had recorded at *MGM Studios* in Orlando to our cousin Phyllis Hyman, who was performing at *The Mann Music Center*, though it appears the demo tape never made it any further than her backstage dressing room. He once took us to *Power 99* FM in hopes that we would make connections in the industry. I've always felt at home on stage. I was petrified at first, but when each performance was over, I wanted more. As previously mentioned, I was a horrible reader in school and I hated reading in front of crowds. I loved public speaking though if I knew the material by heart. I read a lot after college while I was preparing to take the teacher's certification exam. It wasn't until then that I became a good reader. I actually received a nearly perfect score on the reading portion of that exam.

The class at the *Tampa Bay performing Arts Center* only lasted the summer, but I had a great time and met some wonderful people. I dated briefly but I found that there was something off about the people in Tampa. I noticed this when I first visited. I just didn't feel good, lively energy from people. I later found out from a close co-worker, that the people seemed mean. They were brusque and not at all refined. I moved there anyway because at the time there seemed to be more clinical research opportunities in Tampa than in Orlando. When I first moved down there, there were even a couple of Clinical /Contract Research Organizations (CRO's) in Tampa though they closed down shortly after I arrived.

Because I had a stable job at Moffitt, I stayed there for about eight years. That was longest I'd been at any job. I'm proud of that. I also began taking scuba diving lessons. Like singing, diving takes a lot of breathing control and cardio strength. In order to get our diving license; we had to swim 900 feet without stopping, float for five minutes straight, then tread water for five. I practiced but had not built up the stamina to swim that distance without stopping. I met someone during the end of conditioning and didn't put too much effort into continuing.

Chapter 12

Apex

I recall watching an interview with authors Greg Beharendt and Liz Tuccillo who wrote the book, *He's Just not That Into You.* They stated (and I am paraphrasing), that as soon as you get your life together, so to speak, along comes someone to ruin it. I wouldn't say my life was entirely together, but this assertion proved to hold a lot of truth. This is when I discovered that happiness is indeed an inside job. Many prominent masters of self-help have posited that you must: "feel good first!" It's the feeling good that allows what you hope for to flow into your life.

We are wired for love and relationships so while I was not actively searching for love at the time, I was open to a romantic relationship. While I was working at the *H. Lee Moffitt Cancer Center* in Tampa, I became friendly with someone there who gave my number to his barber. One night in late January, I received a call from an unidentified number. I didn't answer. The person then called me back and left a message. I'll call him Kevin...Kevin and I talked for about two hours that evening and stayed in communication for about a month before seeing each other for the first time.

We only lived about 30 minutes away from each other and I later learned that it was pretty odd for a guy who lived so close not to suggest we see each other sooner. I didn't pay much attention to it at the time because we had just met and I was busy traveling, attending church activities, preparing for an exam, and other activities. Plus, while I wasn't dating anyone, I was talking to other guys on the phone. After all, I was 35 at the time so of course I was thinking of marriage and didn't want to rule anyone out.

I later learned, that Kevin purposely refrained from seeing me because he wanted to talk to me for a while prior to meeting me in person. He told me later: "I knew that I would draw you in." I remember hearing Bishop Dale Bronner, a pastor in Atlanta, GA, say something along these lines: a man enters a woman's heart through her ear gates and a woman enters a man's heart through his eye gates. Nevertheless, I learned that if a man draws out the talking, he's most likely trying to hide something. And that's okay. ---You just have to decide if you're willing to deal with that.

I already called myself falling love with him prior to seeing him in person, partially because of our shared family trauma and love for the Lord. As a result of these commonalities, I thought: "Finally!" We went on our first date in early March 2010. I was half an hour late on purpose because I wanted to "punish" him for not seeing me in person sooner (I know right? The games people play). I texted him when I arrived and he was waiting for me at the bar. We were seated then we ate and talked. He would make fun of me months later, saying, "she tore that steak up; my baby can eat!" It's true. Sometimes my table manners can be lacking, but I knew he was teasing me with all his exaggerating. We shared a similar sense of humor.

After we ate, he got in my car and we drove to the Channelside District, a happening spot in Tampa. It features multiple levels filled with clubs, restaurants, a movie theater, bowling, and other attractions. We went dancing then met back at the restaurant to get into our respective cars to go home. As he got out of my car to get into his, he asked me to get out of my car as well so I could give him a hug. I said, "I have to get out to give you a hug?" He said, "yeah...how else are you going to give me a hug goodbye." I got out of my car and noticed a Bible lying on his back seat. Obviously, if you're a regular church attendee, you will most likely have a Bible in your car, as did I, but I'd never dated anyone who seemed to be on the same level as me in terms of our faith. Again, I thought, "this is it!" I was very happy then I got in my car and drove home.

As I was driving home, he sent me a text message stating, "you are the one." I had been hoping he felt the same way I did. We continued talking on the phone that week and on Wednesday he asked me out on a date to a comedy show. We met up at the *Straz Center of the Performing Arts* on Saturday evening. I met some of his friends and we watched the show. At this point, I suppose we were dating. I believe it was the next week he asked me, "will you be my girlfriend?" I'm old fashioned so I thought that was appropriate. He had made it official.

After that, we had a whirlwind romance. We went on many dates to the casino, restaurants, local beaches, and out of town activities. We spent time together doing mundane things like going to Wal-Mart, Target, and just hanging out on Sundays, and after work. Either he was at my house or I was at his. He called just about every morning and wanted to talk to me while I was on my way to work. I'm not a morning person so this was not a particularly welcome occurrence for me. He was offended at first, until I explained to him that I don't really like talking in the mornings. I felt that having to explain that to appease him was kind of a waste of time. It just seemed odd. I didn't like the feeling of having to justify myself, though I understood that he couldn't have known, otherwise. I just got the sense that having to defend myself was the beginning of some type of manipulation or control. He also wanted to talk to me and know of my whereabouts throughout the day. At first, like many women in that situation, I was flattered, thinking, "wow...he cares about me so much."

One day, he tried to make me feel guilty for not calling him the day before. It actually made me feel as though I'd done something wrong and I remember that I didn't like feeling that way. That's when I began to see another side of him that I didn't particularly care for.

He started to blame me for things and tried to make me feel guilty on multiple occasions. The relationship became either hot and cold. As you spend time with a person you will see their true colors probably within the first three months of knowing them. You can either choose to deal with it or leave. We were both still on cloud nine at that time however so my judgment was somewhat clouded.

I had never been in such an emotionally charged relationship. I kept my antennae up because I knew these negative insinuations were new for me as far as romantic relationships are concerned, particularly since my previous boyfriend had set the bar so high. This new relationship, was proving to be an outlier in more ways than one. Two months into it, I was done. We were in the mall and he initiated another verbal altercation. It was just too much. We stopped talking for about three days. Then he told me he would go to counseling both individually and as a couple. I had already been going to therapy in regards to adjusting to my new move and the end of my full-time mom status. It's hard to adjust to focusing on yourself when your life has revolved around someone else for so long. Many mothers lose their identity and have trouble regaining it. This is called a Phase of Life condition and can cause a little depression and some anxiety so I was trying to stay ahead of it.

We started seeing my therapist as a couple. After some of the sessions we went out to dinner. I must admit, we initially felt closer after each session. We only went to about three sessions in total. I really believed he needed to go to counseling on his own. In Michelle Obama's book *Becoming*, she describes her counselor and counseling experience perfectly. She wrote, "he was an empathic and patient listener, coaxing each of us through the maze of our feelings, separating out our weapons from our wounds." Further, she stated that her counselor questioned them in a way that got them to think hard about why they felt a certain way. This empowers us to come up with our own solutions. This is counseling in a nutshell and is a healthy way to navigate life.

We continued our relationship and he eventually came to Philly to meet my family. We also went to New York and Baltimore. We visited several of the amusement parks in Orlando, including The Holy Land Experience. In July, we went on a weekend cruise to Key West. I was really embarrassed as I was "sick as a dog" that weekend. My allergies were in full swing. I don't think I had two minutes free of sneezing the entire weekend. I was miserable. We tried to enjoy ourselves anyway.

During our courtship there were many ups and down, highs and lows. I wasn't accustomed to this in a romantic relationship. All of my previous romantic relationships were emotionally stable. Initially, we went to both his church and then my church on Sundays, eventually settling on my church. We also went to Wednesday night Bible Study. We loved the simple things; going to the beach or a private pier to watch the ripples in the bay. We went to the beach with our families, my son included, when he came to visit. We also loved eating crab legs while watching *Real Housewives of Atlanta*.

We were in love. He later said that he loved our relationship because it was pure and the best relationship he'd ever had. He started going to counseling on his own. I made him go to the doctor and take his blood pressure medication regularly. His mother thanked me for "staying on top of him," to which I replied: "I'm trying." She understandingly replied, "I know." After all, I didn't just love him, I was in love with him.

In August we went on a Royal Caribbean Cruise of the Eastern Caribbean. Many arguments ensued. Despite the counseling, he had become very jealous and controlling. Nonetheless, we stayed together (just barely). The relationship steadily weakened after the cruise and he broke up with me (again) on Thanksgiving eve. Mentally, I was done with him prior to that, but I was still in love with him. He wanted to continue with Thanksgiving dinner but I was done with the roller coaster ride upon which he insisted I was the cause for all of our troubles. I knew I wasn't because I had never been through anything like that before. I didn't want to attend Thanksgiving dinner but he insisted, saying his family was expecting me. I guess he wanted to save face because frankly, I didn't think he wanted to be in the relationship anymore either (for that day, anyway). I went to his house for dinner, and prepared part of the meal. His family and my mother came over. We had an argument that night after everyone left then we broke up and I went home. That was the end of an eight-month relationship.

It turned out to be the heaviest and most dysfunctional romantic relationship I'd ever been in. It was a passionate one and I later learned through biblical scholarship that "passion" is not necessarily a good thing. It has been romanticized throughout the years because of Hollywood, but in biblical terms it means *"suffering."* One thing for sure, I learned more about life and myself during that relationship than I had in the previous 34 years.

The day after Thanksgiving I did not eat at all. Instead, I cried all day long. I allowed myself to have a full day of mourning, though it ended up lasting for years. That Saturday, I gathered myself together and went to my place of solace: Barnes & Nobles. I've always loved the energy there. I was in search of information. "What's wrong with me?" I thought. I wanted the God of the universe to guide me to a book or books that would provide me with the answer. I started reading anything I could get my hands on that might inform me of what I needed to correct my perceived faults. As you read, not only do you get answers that help you understand yourself better, but no matter the topic, life just begins to reveal itself to you and then suddenly, things begin to make sense.

Good leaders are generally always reading something. Your job is to get about reading anything you can get your hands on, otherwise, you don't know what you don't know. Anyway, as I sat in Barnes & Nobles, I was hoping to be pointed in the right direction, hoping a book meant just for me to read that day would maybe fall off the shelf or something. I walked past the Christian books a few times. I briefly read through a book written by T.D. Jakes, discussing his sister and how she was single past the "expected" age for a woman to be married. Reading that made me feel a little better as the story reinforced that I wasn't the only one. But, still, I was looking for more.

I swear I walked past the same section at least three times but didn't see this particular book until it finally stood out among the rest as if it were begging me to pick it up and read it. That book was *As a Woman Thinketh* by Dorothy Hulst. It is a small 64-page book that I still have in my library to this day. I thought, "perfect, I can read this little book real fast," so I sat down and started reading. I was so thirsty for knowledge. Among the many pearls of wisdom the book offers, the author asserts that circumstance does not make the woman; it reveals her. And, "women do not attract that which they want but that which they are." The book asserts that a woman cannot hide her thoughts; they rapidly crystallize into habit. And those habits become circumstances. It was while reading the next part that tears began streaming down my face. The book explains what specific thoughts crystallize into which specific circumstances. I was tearful, not because I was sad, but because of the truth and the revelation. It hit me when I read that thoughts of fear, doubt, and indecision crystallize into weak, unwomanly habits which solidify into circumstances of failure, indulgence, and slavish dependence. I realized that I'd been living in fear. Fearful that I would lose my job or home, caused me to not speak up during meetings at work and being passive in the work environment, was a tactic just so I could stay employed. It was as if I was projecting that I was just glad someone had hired me.

I'd become timid over the years because my power had been taken away. I didn't have any family on which to depend. If I had lost my home, especially while raising my son, we would've been out on the street. I couldn't live with any of my family without being talked about "like a dog." I lived this way and still struggled with it because I didn't have backing or a support system. It's hard, nearly impossible to "go it alone" and be successful. I depended on jobs simply as a way to "stay afloat." I'd put up with so much from a boyfriend, simply because I was away from my family and my support system (which was my church back home at the time). Even though he wasn't good for me I just wanted to be in a relationship so that I wouldn't be alone. This is why I clung to the thought of being with him even after it was clear that we should part ways.

The book I discovered that day became a "must have" for me. It's a spinoff of the men's version: *As a man Thinketh* by James Allen, which I later bought for my son. We know that our thoughts create our life. That is why it is important to give our children the best life possible while raising them, instilling in them a healthy sense of self-esteem and a healthy self-image so they don't have to unlearn adverse ideals in their adult years. Dr. Robin L. Smith, the author of *Lies at the Altar: The Truth About Great Marriages*, suggests that adulthood is our chance to repair the damage done to us in our childhood. Lucky are those who don't have to spend most, if not all of their adult life repairing damage.

Before the night was over, I read another book from the psychology section that I felt described the other individual in the relationship perfectly. Because of my childhood, at times I still struggle with my thoughts and with staying positive. I try to keep before me, Philippians 4:8 (KJV), "Finally, brethren, whatsoever things are true, whatsoever things are honest, whatsoever things are just, whatsoever things are pure, whatsoever things are lovely, whatsoever things are of good report; if there be any virtue, and if there be any praise, think on these things." Also, "casting down imaginations and every high thing that exhalteth itself against the knowledge of God, and bringing into captivity every thought to the obedience of Christ" (2 Corinthians 10:5, KJV). Indeed, we are to cast down any negative thoughts that fail to bring glory to God.

I left the library that evening momentarily fulfilled. I knew however, that my life was never going to be the same. After all, before things unraveled, Kevin and I had a really great time hanging out doing fun things. It was nice and though I knew we could no longer be together, I was obviously going to miss the good parts of the relationship. I heard somewhere that when you go through heartbreak you really begin to understand the meaning behind certain songs. It was during this time that I could relate to *Rocket Love* by Stevie Wonder. I also became aware of what devastation truly meant and the meaning of the "rug being pulled out from under you." Because I'd been a single mom with my main focus on raising my son, I didn't have much experience with romantic relationships. I had sacrificed my social life to be a good mother. Also, I hadn't been in love with anyone since I was 25 years old.

When the relationship had finally ended with my high school sweetheart at age 25, I was very sad but I was not devastated because the break up was gradual and the high wasn't as high nor were the lows as low. That relationship was more stable emotionally. I also understood the term, "lock, stock and barrel" more closely. Kevin had me all to himself. I had no children that would necessarily influence the relationship on a day-to-day basis. I was comfortable financially. I had freedom. I was gainfully employed. I was young and cute (if I do say so myself). I had no ties. I was light and free and he had it all. He had me lock, stock and barrel. I was a good catch yet I still questioned: "am I not enough?" Strange how we come down on ourselves at such times. After all, he was the controlling and manipulative one who harbored insecurities which he projected onto me.

Well, 2010 went on and I continued going to my job and traveling for work, but at the end of each day, I couldn't wait to get home so I could cry my eyes out. I remember being constantly misty eyed. I cried at the drop of a hat. I still had friends from my dance group and my performing arts group and I still went out with them from time to time. For New Year's Eve, I went to a party at my dear friend Sonya's house. Other than that, I continued reading anything I could get my hands on. I had the urge to cut off all my hair, as many women do after a devastating breakup, but I stayed strong. I liked the length of my hair so I got highlights and got it cut into layers instead. I've always had natural highlights but from time to time I would get blonde highlights to give my look a lift.

In January 2011, I had a monitoring visit in Puerto Rico. My new supervisor Leah Santos and I went together. We monitored one of *Moffitt's* studies at *The University of Puerto Rico at Ponce*. Leah told me she is half Cuban and half Irish but that she was born in Puerto Rico. We spent a week there monitoring two studies. I still felt like an imposter but I was always grateful for the experiences. Leah drove us through the mountains and along the winding highways from San

Juan to Ponce. Thank goodness because I would've been so lost trying to read the highway signs and not knowing how to fill up the gas tank, not to mention going through the process of retrieving the car rental in the first place. I'm sure I would have managed in the end, but it was good to have her take the lead.

While on this week-long trip, Leah imparted so much knowledge and wisdom to me that my head started spinning. I knew that I would later write about it. Among so many other things she's the one who first told me that, "all believing equals receiving whereas fear is believing in reverse." We visited the sites of Ponce and lived like the locals for a week. Leah expressed that many Puerto Rican men have a machismo attitude and that it can be hard to get them to settle down, but that Sundays are considered family days. We spent a Sunday at the beach, where we decided to have lunch, and it was full of families enjoying family time.

A couple of weeks later, some friends invited me out for a night of Salsa dancing which I loved. I could really hold my own on the dance floor with a good lead, of course. While I enjoyed, self-reflection and traveling, I needed to socialize. I joined *John Casablanca Modeling and Career Center.* During that time Kevin and I went out to dinner once but he never really made a serious and consistent effort to get me back so I carried on with my life. I'm old-fashioned. I tend to follow the man's lead as that's the way I like it. I continued to attend

Bible-Based but it started to get weird, seeing him there. Therefore, I found a "spinoff" of Bible-Based. One of the former members had started his own little church. There were only about 20 members but it was like the intimate family that I needed at that time.

I joined an elite modeling agency, Jon Casablancas, which is usually meant for teens, however, they had an adult class for women 21 and up. The theme was essentially about carrying yourself like a lady. We were taught how to apply make-up, what things a woman should always have (stockings, camisoles, etc.). We were schooled on effective skin-cleansing regimens, applying the proper colors for your skin tone and many other lady-like secrets. We had a photo shoot and learned how to "smile with our eyes." We also put on a runway show. It was sort of like finishing school if you will. I met two dear friends that I still keep in touch with to this day. I joined a *Zumba* class and found my "home." I absolutely love *Zumba* and Tiffany Waters was the best *Zumba* instructor anyone could ask for. It was there that I met one of my best friends, Desiree Blu. In my adult life, she taught me what real friendship is and she seemed to genuinely like me.

We had lots of fun going to Caribbean parties and other events together. I was involved in social events with my job where I met people and I would attend events with them outside of work. I dated a bit but nothing serious. When I'm in a relationship, I'm in it for real and unfortunately, I was still in love with Kevin. It's always in the back of my mind that every relationship is going to lead to marriage. I remember a surreal my moment when I was on a date with a gentleman sailing the beautiful river at Weeki Wachee Springs. In my mind I wished so badly that it was Kevin sitting next to me instead. I was hoping that when I looked over, I would see him and that the last year or so had just been a bad dream. I looked to my left but he wasn't there, instead it was the other gentlemen. My heart sunk.

Later in 2011, I joined another *Meetup* group to extend my social circle. We had fun. We would go to lunch, dinner, the beach, and other events. It was more like a sorority, however; very cliquish. I'm so much of an individualist, that it didn't really work for me long term. You had to "follow the leader" so to speak and I wasn't with that. I started a "Philly in the Bay" *Meetup*, but the people who joined weren't my crowd so I relinquished the group to a successor. For my birthday that year, I treated myself to a spectacular trip to *LA, Vegas*, and *The Grand Canyon* by way of *Joshua Tree National Forest* and *The Hoover Dam*. I went with my sister and a co-worker. To this day, Vegas is one of my favorite vacation destinations.

In lieu of cutting off all my hair, I opted to get one last relaxer in February 2011 then let my hair grow out naturally. It was a long process. I wore my hair in twists but it became a challenge because the ends still had product in them. Finally, on January 13, 2013, I did it: "the big chop." I haven't quite found out where the urge

142

to cut off one's hair after a crisis comes from but I always think about Job in the Bible when it comes to this. He was going through such a crisis, one of the urges he had, and followed through with, was to cut off all of his hair. It seems that the urge to cut off one's hair has something to do with hair holding some sort of negative energy. Cutting off your hair not only gets rid of the bad energy experienced during the crisis, but it seems to let your brain breathe and you can kind of start over. I'm not sure. I remember a song from a commercial from when I was a kid where the woman was in the shower, singing, *I'm Gonna Wash That Gray Right Outta my Hair* taken from a song, *I'm Gonna Wash That Man Right Outta my Hair.* It wasn't until I got older that I understood it.

During this time, I pursued, my first love once again: musical theater. A passage in the book *As a Woman Thinketh* states, "humanity cannot forget its dreamers; it cannot let their ideals fade and die; it lives in them; it knows them as the realities which it shall one day see and know." What God has placed in your heart will come to pass one way or another because it is His plan for you. It is who you are. I starred as one of the wives in *The King and I* (as well as the sun and a tree). Of course, I just loved it. Acting is a lot of work as there are so many rehearsals. I was doing this as well as working and traveling for work. I was waiting and searching for a production of *Grease* or *The Little Shop of Horrors*. It had been my dream to star in both these plays since I was a kid. I saw a few auditions for those productions but they were too far from where I lived and worked so I had to let that go for the time being.

I love animals and due to my need to nurture, I bought two cats. I had to eventually get rid of them because I traveled so much for work. I knew it was time when I arrived home from a monitoring visit after being away for three days only to find one of my cats locked in my room with the door shut. He'd had no access to food or water. I always shut all of the doors, leaving food and water around in different corners when I went away so they (Smokey and Teena) wouldn't poop on my bed because they were mad at me. But this one time I guess "Smokey" was hiding in my room when I'd shut all the doors and I didn't realize it. I felt horrible and as soon as possible, I surrendered the cats, taking them back to the shelter. I traveled a lot during this time for work and about three times a year, I went home to Philly. My son and grandson also came down to visit me in Florida a couple of times. And later on, just my grandson would come down a couple of times a year.

Chapter 13

Spiritual Awakening

In April 2013, another turning point in my life occurred. After multiple weeks of bible study with Leah at work, she invited me and two other members of our bible study group to a biblical scholarship class with the theme *Abundant Living.* The class teaches accurate knowledge of The Word of God with the aim of increasing the power of God in the attendees' lives. The class met three days a week for four weeks. This was an amazing experience and I learned so much. The following are some of those revelations:

- There is a law of believing that says: you say it, you believe it; God will bring it to pass.
- Fear always makes us less than what we are supposed to be.
- Belief is a verb, a belief manifests through actions.
- Never bring God's word down to your level. Bring your beliefs up to what the word says. Don't rely on what you can conceive. Rely instead on what the word of God says.

We also learned that all scripture interprets itself in the verse, the context, or where it was used elsewhere in the Bible. It is not to be left up to private interpretation. We learned how to break up terms like Holy Spirit using Greek (pneuma hagion). We learned many other words that were Latin derivatives leading to a better understanding of the word and the power gained by knowing how to rightly divide the Word of God. We learned that "Theo-ph-i-lus" in Acts really means "the beloved of God." Many people think that is referring to a city (The former treatise have I made, O Theophilus...). We are the beloved of God so this is addressed to us.

The climax of the class came when we learned Colossians 1:27, when God would make known what is the riches of the glory of this mystery among the Gentiles; which is <u>Christ in you</u>, the hope of glory (KJV). Christ means the anointed one. He performed many miracles in His day. This Christ lives within each of us if we receive Him and all of the miracles he performed; we can perform them, too. It says so in the verse. The significance of this is that in order for us to receive this secret, Jesus had to be crucified and the Holy Spirit had to come; but the enemy would not have crucified Jesus had he known that so many would receive this power. When we learned this, you could almost hear thunder and some huge breakthrough in the heavens. It was profound. My life didn't do a 180-degree change but after learning all of this I felt so empowered and grateful that I was armed with so much knowledge which would ultimately help me to work toward living a more purposeful life.

Time went on and I had grown so much and felt much more empowered, however, I still couldn't shake wanting to be with my ex. I think that relationship was so impactful because it was my first relationship as an adult where I was carefree, happy, and financially comfortable. I could really put time into a relationship for the first time in a long time. Plus, Kevin had put his best foot forward in the beginning, which is the Kevin I had fallen in love with. In some ways, I was probably more in love with wanting to be in love than I was with Kevin himself. After all, we had a lot of fun and really enjoyed just hanging out in the beginning and I wanted that feeling back.

I remember driving to work one morning thinking about all this and feeling mournful. I heard a voice from deep down in my gut say, "Karima, look at all the growth you've had since the breakup...isn't that why you moved down here? You're never going to get back with Kevin again...but it's because of that devastating breakup that you sought all this information, allowing you to grow so much. Unbeknownst to him, he'd played a part in my journey. His time in your life is over." It was such a clear message and it made sense. And that was that. I wouldn't dwell on it anymore.

A couple of years later I became a certified *Zumba* instructor. I seemed to be getting recognition by my peers for my fitness and athleticism as well as for my verbal skills, and writing abilities. It is important to be alert to those skills your peers come to you for leadership with. Those are your gifts. I then decided to attend broadcasting school in Tampa as my childhood aspiration of becoming a news anchor had never left me. I had to explore it once and for all. Many in the class dropped out and only two people were left, with one of them being me, but there was no real momentum or good energy left.

I started graduate school in August of 2014, pursuing my Master's in Professional Counseling. I had been through so much and learned so much and I knew I had done the work to overcome many of my obstacles. I had to share it with others so they could learn from my mistakes. And, "we know that all things work together for good to them that love God, to them who are the called according to his purpose" (Romans 8:28).

It became my dream to open a not-for-profit Community Counseling Center in my hometown of Philadelphia. There I would provide counseling services, etiquette classes, and Zumba lessons, sort of like a finishing school. I also wanted to have a radio talk show like Dr. Joy or work on T.V. like Dr. Jen. I started grad school but I had to take a short pause to finish broadcasting school. This time, I attended The Connecticut School of Broadcasting in Orlando, FL. During that time, my employer let me work from home meaning I didn't have that three-hour a day commute.

The classes only lasted four months and then I received my certificate. In my opinion, those schools aren't bad as long as you have a back-up plan and other education, a foundation of basic academic skills if you will.

I continued grad school in the fall of 2015. I resigned from my job on good terms January 2016, to concentrate on grad school because at the rate I was going, it seemed I would be in school forever. I wanted to get out of school and get on to my counseling career and all the great things I would accomplish in this world. Those lofty goals proved elusive for some time. I lived off of my retirement for a year and a half. All of 2016, I stayed in my apartment while attending school. I paid all of my bills with my retirement. In February, I took myself on a trip to Greece where I met a group of single young ladies and we really had a good time. I tried to remain in my apartment but felt it was time to leave Tampa.

Although, I'd made many good friendships in Tampa, I was lonely because I was spending more time alone than ever before as I was no longer going into work. I'd also stopped going to church. As you will see, I ended up paying for this isolation in the years to follow. My pastor at Bible-Based passed away and then the pastor at another church that I was attending also passed. The preaching at the Bible-Based "spinoff" church had started to not quite sit right with me. I began attending *Christian Family Fellowship*, the fellowship Leah was a part of. I continued to learn a lot about the Bible. We went to an event in Destin, FL which was beautiful, but overall, the group attendees were not my peers. I focused on grad school, continuing to see some friends, and attending *Zumba* classes. Many of the people that were in Tampa early on had moved away. It was just about that time to move on...

Chapter 14

What's in a Name?

"Oh, that though wouldst bless me indeed" (1 Chronicles 4:10). I love this Bible verse. It is part of The Prayer of Jabez. He was named Jabez because his mother bore him with much sorrow. It is the story of an individual with a sad past and no hope for the future or acceptance by his fellow man. The prayer of Jabez is as follows:

> And Jabez called on the God of Israel, saying, Oh, that though wouldst bless me indeed, and enlarge my coast, and that thine hand might be with me, and that though wouldst keep me from evil, that it may not grieve me! And God granted him that which he requested.

The scripture reminds us that sometimes, where there is much sorrow in the beginning, the sequel will be the exact opposite in the latter days. Job 8:7 reveals that "though thy beginning was small, yet thy latter end should greatly increase." Johnathan 61:3 tells us that "God will give us beauty for ashes." One of my mentors once told me that just as far as the roots of the tree go into the ground that is how far your blessings extend. Finally, I heard another philosopher compare this phenomenon to a bow and arrow. The further you feel life pulling back, that's the exact distance you will leap forward in a positive direction. *The Prayer of Jabez* by Charles Sturgeon states that "to a great extent we find we must sow in tears before we can reap in joy." He goes on to assert that, "you may expect God's blessings if you continue to persevere under many discouragements."

The Bible doesn't make any mention of Jabez changing his name but he did end up being a very blessed man. This just speaks to the importance of a name and how it can shape your destiny. God's blessings are effectual.

I was born when my dad was 42 years old. I was his first child. He was born in 1931 and his siblings were born somewhere around that time too, having their children in the 1950's and 60's. All of his siblings had children long before I was born in 1974 so I was everyone's "baby." In regards to my personality as a child, most people on my dad's side usually had positive things to say. On my mom's side, it was a different story. While no one said anything outright bad to me, I've heard bad things said about me. I also get the sense that I was viewed as an intruder in some way. Some in my mother's family were not very fond of my father for various reasons. When I came along it seems the family on my mom's side kind of felt like I did not really belong in their family. No one came out and said it but I always felt like an outsider. Perhaps, that was just a reflection of my mother's guilt, in some way, about stepping outside of the family mindset.

These are the unspoken codes or beliefs Goldenberg and Goldenberg (2013) mention in their text *Family Therapy*. They assert that every family has them. They are not verbalized; it's just "the way we do things." They explain this concept as narratives and assumptions and state that "a family is a maker of meaning." They go on to state that "our individual judgment about what constitutes reality is a function of the beliefs and stories that the family imparts about their experiences." Moreover, they say that throughout the course of this thought process, a family fashions and helps instill fundamental and enduring assumptions about the world in which it lives. Consequently, the meanings and understanding we attribute to events and situations we encounter are embedded into the family's social, cultural, and historical experiences. This is very delicate and usually, not to be disturbed. I tend to think that subconsciously, some may have thought I disturbed this delicate balance of the family mindset of keeping up a middle-class image.

Stephen Covey mentions, in his book, *The 7 Habits of Highly Effective People* that most of society places most of their existence on their image. My mom was raised in a middle-class family. For the most part, her family was on the lighter side of the brown-skinned spectrum. Her two older siblings carried on that middle-class legacy, occupationally, and had two children each;

a boy and a girl. My mom (the youngest) followed suit. She too had two "light-skinned" kids by her first husband; a boy and a girl. She met my dad and had a brown-skinned child, out of wedlock. Perhaps her family felt I'd "messed-up" their delicate balance. Though I do believe that some of them realized: "it's not the child's fault." Though I'm not certain of that as I always had the sense that my mom was kind of ashamed of me in regards to whether or not I fit it with, or would be accepted by her side of the family. I felt I was to remain hidden.

Even though people don't tell me very many stories of my childhood, I do have a vivid memory of it. I remember my personality as a child and my childhood as if it were yesterday. I was a good kid even though I was loud, talkative, and mischievous. I loved life and prior to having my son, I felt that I was in control of my life.

I taught myself this lesson when I was seven and my older sister was 17 and she got the chicken pox. When I was seven, my 17-year-old sister got the chicken pox. I remember thinking, "when I'm 17 I'm supposed to want boys to like me and I do not want to look like that then." I must have overheard someone say that once you get the chicken pox you cannot get them again. What I considered to be a smart and courageous move, I sat next to my sister on purpose so I too could get infected with the chicken pox. It was at that my moment that I knew I controlled what happened to me in my life and I remember feeling a tinge of power. Later on, that confidence was taken away but I later got it back which is why I'm where I am today. "Therefore, do not throw away your confidence, which has a great reward. For you have need of endurance, so that when you have done the will of God you may receive what is promised." (Hebrews 10:35-36, *KJV*)

Allender (2005) discusses the importance of your name in his book, *To be Told*. He says that a name is chosen to reflect the unique calling and character of a child. My father is Muslim. I have an Arabic first and middle name. No one on my mother's side had an Arabic name when I was growing up. I never hated my name but it was just another thing that set me apart from everyone else on my maternal side of the family. Whereas many of my cousins on my dad's side had such names.

Allender says "our name is our identity." It is interesting. I was looked down on a lot as a kid by family members and by some teachers. Because I was not adequately nurtured for a large part of my life, my name became associated with someone scolding me in some way, starting out at home and then in school. To this day, in social situations, when I hear my name, I sometimes tense up, just hoping that something positive follows. It is because of this that I considered changing my name.

That bad breakup in 2010 was the catalyst for deeper soul-searching which really led me to consider changing my name. After the break up, I became so entrenched in the Word of God and the desire to understand it that I thought; "I am a new person now, I don't want that name anymore, I want a biblical name." I seriously considered changing my name to Sarah. This way, when I heard someone calling my name there wouldn't be any more anxiety attached to it.

There are many examples in the Bible where God changed people's names and subsequently their lives changed for the better. I am feeling this could be true for me as well. Also, I recall Iyanla Vanzant (who also changed her name) stating that your name has a spirit attached to it. I believe that though I'm not sure of the scientific or spiritual meaning behind it. Whenever someone's name was changed in the Bible, a blessed life soon followed. Allender (2005) states, that the Bible tells us, that those who seek God will one day be given a new name. My reluctance however continues to be that Karima (generous) Safiya (pure) is such a beautiful name that it would be hard to find something more beautiful. I would have to find something with a deeper meaning. My dad really did a good job picking out that name.

Below is what is mentioned in the book by Charles Surgeon as it pertains to Jabez' desires for his blessings. But I would like to think about it in regards to selecting a name. If I were to change my name, I would like to factor in the following:

"Let the grace of God prompt it; let the bounty of God confer it; and then the endowment shall be something godlike; something worthy of the lips that pronounce the benediction, and verily to be craved by everyone who seeks honor that is substantial and enduring".

Chapter 15

The Messy Middle

In March 2017 (almost 8 years to the day), I packed up my apartment in Tampa, gave away my furniture, packed up my car, and got on the road towards Orlando. I must admit that I've done some pretty courageous things in my time. As T.D. Jakes would say, "I felt the fear and did it anyway." That is true courage. I decided I was going to stay in a hotel in the Orlando area until I finished grad school. I just had to get out of Tampa. Too many memories and the town's energy had diminished.

By moving to the Orlando area, at least I would be closer to family. By then, my mom lived half an hour north of Orlando and I had some cousins there too. In my opinion the energy in the city of Orlando was much more upbeat than that of Tampa. My ultimate goal at that point was to make my way back home to Philly. Staying in a fairly decent hotel would cost me about $1,300 a month and at the time that was out of my price range. I stayed at an Extended Stay for a month, before I reluctantly moved in with my mom. I was really embarrassed; here I was 41 years old and living with my mother. I thought, "how will this look?" Here I am moving in with my mother at this age and my offspring doesn't even live with me. I would like to say that I didn't care what people thought but I did. I thought and felt like I was going backwards.

By moving in with my mother, I felt like I was jeopardizing my integrity. After all the soul-searching I'd done, I felt like I was selling my soul. I felt like I was at the lowest point of my life. I understand that many wouldn't see anything wrong with this, particularly as it was just a temporary move. We all know that it's not ideal to live with a parent at that age but how bad could it be? For me, it was terrible. After all, it had taken me years of deprogramming and reframing my identity to get to a place of wholeness. My mom hadn't actually raised me and furthermore, she did as much as she could to destroy me, but here I was under that negative energy again...

I had accomplished so much in spite of all she had and hadn't done. I wanted to continue my independence, relying on myself and God. At least living that way, although I faced obstacles, my day-to-day life was somewhat orderly. In my mind, here I was "crawling" back (at least it felt like it looked that way). In my Family Therapy class, I learned of a family dynamic where an abusive parent targets one (perhaps the one they feel is the weakest or who has no other support), leaving them feeble and dependent on them. That way, the child always has to depend on that parent thus the parent never needing to be alone.

Looking back at some of my past, I started to notice such a pattern. It had occurred to me for a while that perhaps she'd wanted me to have a child so that I would have to continue to depend on her. She kept me as her dependent, failing to inform me about services that could help me become independent, even though she worked in social services. I desperately wanted my independence.

I recall being 18 and saving up all my checks then fleeing to the bank to open up an account for myself. I really felt that she was trying to stifle my growth in the hopes that she could hold me captive so to speak. And I thought, "wow...it took a while but I'd subconsciously fallen right into that pathological, familiar dynamic." I knew that I wasn't weak and I knew this wouldn't be my end result for I was now well aware of how intelligent, strong, resourceful, and independent I had become, but it happened anyway. I was nauseated at the thought of it. And what would other people say or think? I know she talks bad about me and always has. I saw it first hand and also heard about it. What would other people think? They would think I was an idiot to move back in with her. They would think that I was trying to win her love. This couldn't be farther from the truth. I always knew I couldn't. I gave up that hope early on in my teen years.

Today, it's hard to say whether or not she loves me. I know she did when I was a little girl and that's all I'm concerned about, because, as I as stated earlier, I at least received something to give me the chemical input needed for fortitude and insight. I gave up hope a long time ago that I would feel love from her. Thankfully, I'd received a foundation and at that point I wasn't trying to win hers or anyone else's love for that matter. Love should be freely given and as Maya Angelou has declared, "Love liberates."

I realized a while ago that a person's core doesn't change. People don't really change foundationally. Dr. Phil talks about this in his book *Life Code*. Either they love you or like you or they don't. People change superficially but their core does not, good, bad, or indifferent. Additionally, I learned in my Family Therapy class that the scapegoat or the child that had been somewhat rejected by the family, was actually rejected before the child was born. Perhaps they are considered an "outside child" or they are considered "illegitimate." Whatever the reason, if the child was rejected for reasons that only the elders in the family know, that child will grow up feeling rejected. The child will feel that no matter what they do, they will never be accepted. The child will inevitably act out in some way. I read an African proverb that I am paraphrasing: a child that is not embraced by the village will end up burning it down to feel its warmth. That's extreme but understood. The child will never be accepted by the family no matter how hard he or she tries because the rejection actually has nothing to do with the child. It has everything to do with the thoughts of how the child will turn out because of the way the parent(s) chose to bring the child into the world. If that child loses their true identity, they will grow up surrounded by all the negative projections from their family and people will fault the child, not realizing that all of these negative feelings were projected onto the child. What does a screen do when it is projected upon? Gives an output of that exact projection. This is very apparent in some parts of my life. Thankfully I had the safeguard of my dad and my school district that had somewhat higher expectations for me. Never fight for anyone's love because their actions will tell you everything you need to know.

For me, in all situations, social or professional, I mirror the person's actions toward me. That is not to say that I don't have my own biases. I was horribly judgmental as a teenager and young adult. But that was because I felt inadequate. I always tried to find flaws in people to lower their status in some way. In my eyes, this made me feel better about myself. I read somewhere that people echo to us publicly what we think of them privately.

A person acts towards us based on our thoughts about them. It is true that our thoughts are broadcast throughout the ether. Your thoughts also come out through your facial expressions and body language. If someone is a particularly good reader of social cues, they will know exactly how you truly feel about them during each interaction.

I'm not mentioning any of this to bring judgment upon anyone. I think people do the best they can, for the most part. Financially, my mom has been there for me 99% of the time. I have come to realize that perhaps due to her own upbringing this has been all that she is capable of. Obviously, I'm only telling my side of the story, my perspective.

I saw a post on social media which read: "You own everything that happened to you. Tell your stories. If people wanted you to write warmly about them, they should have behaved better." But that is the point. And that goes for me too; if my name were to be mentioned in someone else's story, it would be evident once again that no one is perfect. Furthermore, if we study the model of Narrative Therapy, we can learn ways to change our story to one where we can become the highest version of ourselves.

In May of 2017, I started my practicum at The Vines Hospital in Ocala, FL, in the women's unit. It was a dream come true. I couldn't see myself doing anything else. It was recognized by the staff, too. I was walking down the hall one morning as one of the managers walked towards me and asked me my name. I told her then she lit up and asked, "are you the intern?" I thought to myself, "that's a good sign; I'm probably being talked about in a positive way." That was rare for me and I wasn't used to it. During our runway performance rehearsal at John Casablanca, when I walked down the runway in my make-up and evening gown, I heard one of the directors say, "what is her name?" Another time when I was at an audition for a make-up airbrush at Home Shopping Network (HSN), one of the casting directors pointed to me and said, "her definitely." I bring these instances up because it's good to be aware of subtle clues that inform you of what others see when they look at you. And the opposite is true when it comes to personal growth, and ways to know, "maybe this isn't for me." It helps to steer you in the right direction or get confirmation that perhaps you are on the right track.

I completed my practicum with The Vines in August of 2017. I was told on multiple occasions, "well, you can always work here," which was good to hear. It can be difficult for a new graduate to be hired at such a highly esteemed hospital without yet being licensed. I had to pay for hotel stays during my weeks at The Vines because I couldn't commute every day from Sanford (where my mom lived), to Ocala, FL.

I didn't really want to move to Ocala however plus I had to move on to my internship. I was almost done with my education. I interviewed for an internship at a youth correctional facility in Kissimmee. I was offered the position however I was reluctant to take it because of the environment. I also interviewed (several times) for an African-American run private practice in Orlando. While still in school, I was promised many opportunities to work within the community, the radio stations, and other extensions of the practice. It was a slow-paced environment as many mental health private practices can be. I was not getting all of the hours I needed so I could not stay. Consequently, I phoned the youth correctional facility to see if they still had an opening. I had to get my internship hours in and get out of school. Thankfully, they were able to accommodate me.

I loved working with the youth there. It was literally the funniest environment I'd ever been a part of. Everybody seemed to be a comedian (employees included). In the long run however, it turned out to be a bit of a toxic environment. I wasn't asked to come back after I'd finished my internship, but I didn't want to anyway. Because I'm humble, people tend to take that as a weakness, therefore, I frequently end up sort of telling somebody off. I don't want to, but everyone has a breaking point. I have come to realize that in many situations and environments, the most toxic person, especially if they have an exaggerated personality, seems to have the most influence. They appear to "run things," at least in the short run, which is usually how long I tend to stick around. Unfortunately, that was the case there and while working in that environment I saw my personality begin to change.

The inmates really do run such institutions. I did have a positive impact on the clients however, as expressed by many of them, and one of the highlights for me, was in teaching one of them to read. I realized that his behavioral problems didn't come from him being a "bad" person; instead, they stemmed from boredom and from being disconnected from society, mainly because he couldn't read. He was 15 and could barely read on a first-grade level. After working with me, he began reading on a third-grade level. He said that he was going to tell his mom, "if I'm going to be here at least I'm learning how to read."

It was now December 2017 and I'd been trying really hard to find a job. I had graduated with my Master's in Professional Counseling but as with most new graduates, I was essentially penniless. I thought, "what has become of my life?" I didn't know where this was going and I was scared. I took a job as a sort of a home health aide worker and a telemarketer.

I was eventually offered a therapist role with an African-American owned private practice. I was really excited to work under their leadership. I would continue my dream of becoming a counselor for not only one but two agencies. Surely, I would eventually recoup all of my losses, right? Something had to change. For some time, I went through ups and downs in finding stable, lucrative employment and there were times where I got discouraged. I have become resilient however and know to keep pressing forward.

In October of 2018, my son's grandmother passed away. My son and grandson had been staying with her. My dad was 87 years-old at the time with declining health. It was at this point that I thought, "it's time for me to move back to Philly." I didn't want my son and grandson in Philly without someone there to look after them. It had been my dad's children's job to take care of him, however, none of them lived in the area anymore. I could not place that burden on his two oldest grandchildren. That's when I understood why I'd had such difficulty finding a permanent position in Florida after grad school. God had other plans for me; it was clearly time for me to move back Philly.

Chapter 16

Back to Philly

I accomplished a great deal while in Florida. I had a successful work-life balance, grew spiritually, finished grad school, explored broadcast journalism, did a lot of travelling, met a lot of people, got involved in performing and dancing and had my own, peaceful apartment. For once I was carefree and able to grow into my own version of Karima. I was no longer defined by family dysfunction and disrespect. Although I still have more growing to do, I'm really happy that I experienced growth on so many levels.

I knew when it was finally time to make my next move, however. Things were no longer falling into place for me and I believe God was nudging me to move on. That being said, I moved back to Philly in October 2018. My plan was to stay at Matthew's grandmother's house so that Matthew and I could split the mortgage and hopefully, eventually keep the house; not for me necessarily but so that he and Johnathan would always have a home. I wanted Matthew and Johnathan to continue in their comfortable lifestyle. Matthew's surroundings had always been comfortable in regards to his home life. He may not have been happy but when he lived with me, his home was always nice, comfortable, peaceful, and clean; and in a nice neighborhood. I felt like that was the least I could provide.

Johnathan was flourishing at Willow Hill Elementary School in Willow Grove, PA. He was involved in all sorts of activities. He even played the trumpet and he was good at it. Johnathan and Matthew had already been through enough instability. I wanted them to live out their lives as comfortably as possible, with the aim of reaching their fullest potential. Additionally, I knew the type of trauma that could come from plucking a child away from a middle-class (even working class) lifestyle into poverty, which I suspected might happen to Johnathan if I didn't step in.

Matthew didn't have the same vision as me however. As you know, our relationship had been strained for the better part of 10 years and he had no desire for me to move in with them, whether I paid the mortgage or not. I had been hoping Matthew would accept my help and put Johnathan's needs above his disdain towards me.

The first day I arrived in Philly, Johnathan and Matthew were happy to see me. It was Halloween and they both came running into the house to check in with me prior to making their rounds. When they arrived, I was taking a nap and let them know I was fine. I soon discovered however that they had bed bugs. Unbeknownst to me, though I'd never even seen a bed bug before, the Philadelphia area had been struggling with this epidemic in recent years. Matthew hadn't been raised with bed bugs or any other vermin while he lived with me. Because I know he loves his son and is truly trying his best, I couldn't understand how he was okay with living with bed bugs where his son was concerned…

I knew I couldn't stay in that house because I would risk carrying them to other places and just the thought of something crawling on me and biting me as I slept creeped me out. Instead, I stayed with my dad that evening and researched bed bug removal companies. I told Matthew that I would help pay for the extermination but he rejected the offer. He was completely irate, stating that I wasn't even staying there with him and Johnathan. I didn't want to stay there anyway because of the bugs but I was willing to do whatever I could in order to ensure Johnathan would remain at his school.

I never stayed there again. Instead, I stayed with my dad in his apartment in the Northeast while I worked at a school down the street. During my last stint staying with my mom in Florida, I felt like I had hit rock bottom, but this was even worse. Here I was staying with my 87-year-old father in senior citizen housing in a studio apartment. Transition periods between cities and jobs can be challenging at first and deep down I knew this was a temporary arrangement, but the environment made me feel like my future was bleak and deteriorating by the day.

I continued working until Christmas break then I flew down to Florida to pick up my car. I had been using my dad's car until then so it felt like things were moving forward when I finally was able to bring my car up north. I put everything else in storage. I asked my son to help but per his usual, he declined. Though I continued working at the school down the street from my dad's place, I was eventually offered a better position at another agency. It was a more professional position, and things were beginning to fall into place. I knew it was time to move out of my dad's.

I asked my sister if she thought one of her friends might like to have a roommate. I was really happy when my sister's friend allowed me to stay with her and her mother in Exton, PA. To protect her identity, I'll call her "Sue." I agreed to pay her $600 per month. I also bought food and other items for myself and the household. Additionally, I gave her extra money for water and electric.

We got along great at first. I left the house every morning to go to work and on weekends, I sometimes went to visit my grandson in Willow Grove. At other times I'd go out with friends after work. Sue and I talked about life, relationships, etc. There came a point however, when Sue and her mother began to ask me to do menial tasks (take this radio downstairs...order this on Amazon for me...hook up the Bluetooth speaker for me...can you clean out the emails from my inbox?...can you pick up this item while you're out?...can you take the trash out?...can you shovel the driveway?...can you pick up my boyfriend-(her mother and I picked up her boyfriend from the train station while Sue cooked and get dolled up for him)-I really didn't mind though-Sue and I were friendly. Of course, I did some things simply because I was staying there. I shoveled sometimes, although I didn't really know how. I'd really never had to do it. When I was younger this was my brother's job, and after I left home, I lived in apartments and in Florida.

We all pitched in but Sue complained about everything. The shoveling wasn't good enough, or the toilet paper I bought was too "flimsy." But in all honesty, I didn't do anything unless it was 100% convenient for me because, after all, I was a working woman who was paying rent. I wasn't an indentured servant and certainly wasn't there mooching off of them rent free.

As time went on, nothing was ever good enough. I diplomatically and tactfully explained how being asked to do all these menial tasks made me feel. At this time, I was also attending to my ailing father. I could tell Sue was offended, however, I needed to speak my mind. These frequent requests had to stop and I felt I had held my tongue long enough. She was very offended and began to give me the silent treatment but the requests ended. I knew it was time to find my own place. I only planned on staying there a few months anyway. I had always been on my own.

By May 5, 2019, I was finally in my new apartment. It had taken almost two years: going from hotel, to my mom's, to my son's grandmother's, to my dad's, to Sues; to finally back on my feet. It's interesting how seamless my move to Florida had been; whereas moving back home to Philly turned out to be an uphill battle, to say the least. Nonetheless, I did what I thought was right for me at the time, plus I felt like I wanted to be closer to my boys. Besides, my dad needed someone to be there if he had an emergency, which he eventually did. In April of 2019 he was found by a cousin lying on the floor unable to move. We almost lost him.

A common theme in my life has been that of rejection. It just seemed like no one ever really wanted me. Was it the energy I was putting out? Was it set in motion because my own parents didn't care enough to raise me? I remember expressing this to a friend in Tampa: that I felt no one cared about me or wanted to help me. She said "you can change that." I remember reading somewhere that a good measure of resiliency is one's ability to tactfully ask for help in a bold manner. It's still difficult for me to ask for help when I need it, though I try to, but when I do I feel like I'm being a burden. This is something I must continue to work on. This is one of the reasons I moved in with my mom in 2017. I thought surely someone has to help me at some point...no one should have to do EVERYTHING alone – we'll see, I thought.

When I moved in with my mom to finish grad school, she left me alone for the most part. However, one day she looked at me and said, "your life is so messed up..." What a horrible thing to say to someone! I couldn't believe she had the audacity to say that to me after all the neglect I had endured as a kid and all of the obstacles I'd faced, many of which she'd purposely put into place to make things more difficult for me. It amazes me when people can't (or won't) admit cause and effect especially when they may have played a role in certain outcomes.

I began to feel like my family was talking disparagingly about me behind my back, further pushing me out into the fringes. I was being treated like an imbecile. It was and is clear to me that "no one cares." I have friends whom I feel love and care about me more than my blood family does. I'd always been kicked around on my mom's side. It was now spreading to my dad's side and possibly being projected in my external world as a whole. I knew that I had to fix something within me. Through consistent self-assessment, I continue to improve and get stronger every day.

I will still keep before me that there are people who do care about me because I have seen this demonstrated through friendships. It remains that it is still difficult for me to ask for help. In grad school while getting my degree in counseling, we learned that healthy "help seeking" is good. I've not yet gotten up the courage to follow this theory, especially since I tested it once or twice and my beliefs were confirmed. In regards to my family, I know I didn't do anything to anyone. It feels like it's just a cancer and I am the target. I'm used to it since I have dealt with it my entire life. I move on with my life however, resting peacefully because I know I haven't done anything to harm anyone. I've just been the scapegoat for everyone else's pain. Therefore, for the most part, I stay away from them and they stay away from me. Unfortunately, this alienation sometimes follows me into the workplace. I'm not sure what people see when they look at me that makes them think they can get away with certain types of disrespect. I'm not a doormat, I'm just not overly assertive. I'm just assertive enough to go for the things that I want out of life. I have no interest in harming anyone to get it. What's mine is mine. I'm pretty much an easy-going person and I'm pretty laid-back.

I will continue to be true to myself and carry myself like a lady with class, although, as demonstrated on more than one occasion, I'm not afraid of confrontation. I just don't feel like living in that space. If an individual and I don't agree or if I feel disrespected, I simply remove myself. I don't feel like fighting. I've been fighting all my life. There are plenty of people who are respectful and do not behave in an offensive way. Those are the people with whom I chose to surround myself. Goldenberg and Goldenberg (2013) mention this in their text *Family Therapy*. They assert that when a person is mistreated within their family, it is often carried over to other environments as this is their first point of reference. The way to check this is to first confront your family. That in turn gives you the power to check individuals outside of your family. I've done this and have no problems doing it, but when the disrespect continues, you eventually realize that it's the individual's issue, not yours. Gracefully remove yourself from the situation and continue living and growing.

My son is included in the distancing. Our relationship is contentious. So far, my grandson still loves me and is open to having a relationship with me. That is what is currently most important to me. As far as my son is concerned, I have apologized a million times to him in terms of his circumstances. I moved away temporarily because I had to. I moved back when I was healed and made myself available for him, Johnathan, and my dad. My son was indirectly taught not to respect me and not to listen to me. He witnessed others mistreating me and talking about me and he saw me somewhat lowering myself to their standards. I had learned to expect mistreatment by many and consequently, my son's and my relationship was strained before I left for Florida. And it is strained now that I'm back. It may always be this way, however I will not stop praying for our continued healing.

I need peace. I am a peaceful person. I have never been a person who was involved in drama, not by choice, anyway. For the most part, I'm a naturally happy person. In Valerie Burton's book, *Successful Women*

Think Differently, she states that about 50 % of happiness is genetic (some people just have a predisposition to be happy), 40 % of happiness is about intentional activity, and 10 percent of your happiness is determined by your circumstances. These numbers suggest that you have to make the choice to be happy. Some people don't have that 50 percent happiness disposition while others do.

Because of the difficulties I experienced in my life, I've had to work extra hard to be happy. But I believe that innately, I have the 50 % innate happiness disposition. I can always find some reason to laugh. This is not to say that I can't be moody because I can, but for the most part I am just a naturally happy person. I'm working on being "lighter" and happier. I'm also spiritual and put my trust in my faith, which helps. Additionally, I'm naturally athletic and love to dance, which also boosts endorphins. My dad has always been fit and my mom was a dancer so I get the athleticism gene from both sides. If I did not have the happiness disposition, I would have given up a long time ago. From my experience the best cure for depression is serving others. You have to take the attention off of yourself. Serving others has been my life's mission. And today, my hope is that my story will encourage others.

I love life and want to experience everything it has to offer me. Prayerfully things will continue to get better. Dr. Phil said that your life should get better as you age because you accumulate experience. I've also read somewhere that a measure of emotional intelligence is the effective ability to adapt well to change. These are just a few things to keep in mind along this journey called life.

Between overseeing my father's care, work, and getting settled in to my life, I've not had much time to socialize, although, I did join a gym and *Toastmaster's* again. I was a member of Toastmaster's in Tampa. It is a public speaking club where you practice public speaking and leadership skills. While participating, I recognized a marked increase in my confidence throughout my daily life.

I even started dating though I didn't last long on the dating scene. I suppose I'm still not ready. When the student is ready the teacher will appear. I want to be married however, and I'm not willing to settle. I don't care how long I have to wait. When the time is right, it will happen. Many of the men I've come in contact with are either separated or recently divorced, and not willing to invest time into getting to know someone authentically; instead, it seems they want to jump right into the bedroom. It also seems they are used to low morals and promiscuity, which doesn't surprise me. It appears that with social media we've become a heavily sexualized generation. I want to tell some of them, "you do know that you can live without having sex, right?" I've been celibate for almost 10 years now, and that's how I plan to stay until I meet that person whom I feel is worth it, hopefully my husband.

I've never been promiscuous and I'm not about to start now. Instead, I find other ways to boost my confidence and then learn to say and do what I want to say in a bold way. One thing I've learned is that when I make a decision, I must stick to it. I read somewhere that successful people make decisions quickly and rarely change their minds, if at all. They don't second-guess their decisions, and don't incorporate anymore emotion into them than what was present at the onset. I've learned to act without spending too much time on what I should do. That's how some amazing situations have come about for me. I look back and say, "I did that?" and before I knew it, it became a part of who I am.

I don't have much of an issue with confidence but I could work on my boldness. I'm naturally soft spoken and don't personally see a problem with that. However, some people only understand boldness but I have learned that you can be bold and soft spoken at the same time, exuding confidence simultaneously.

Michelle Obama speaks about this in her book *Becoming*, stating that Valerie Jarrett has this exact demeanor; a manner about herself that you have no choice but to respect. She speaks softly but with boldness, looking you right in the eye. One can pray for boldness and confidence, and exercise, run, and read books on the subject which helps. Maya Angelou said that the words we choose and the points we make with those words can be powerful. I suggest reading about the subject that you are concerned about and apply your learning to your life. "Faith without works is dead" (James 2:24, *NKJV*). And "words become flesh" (John 1:14, *KJV*).

I never thought I would struggle so much to get married. I thought marriage would be the next step after graduating from college at twenty-three. I imagined myself married by twenty-five. I thought it would just happen. Because I didn't get married when I thought I would, my life seemed to het harder and more difficult to navigate. I've learned the power of words and more than ever I purposely speak positivity into my life and my life is getting easier. My desires are coming more easily to me. Motivational speaker Kevin Trudeau asserts that, "what you want, wants you." I now believe that. Hence, I'm looking forward to walking into all of the blessings already written into the story of my life.

Marriage was never really discussed with me growing up. No one "prepared" me to be a wife. I've heard friends tell me that they were repeatedly told: "when you become a wife" or "this is how to keep your husband happy." These things were never mentioned to me. I always thought I would be married. I thought it would just be the natural progression of normal development; graduate from high school, then college, then get married. It didn't work out that way for me however. I simply wasn't prepared or groomed for such. However, through research and observation of friends and mentors, I've learned a lot about marriage. I've come to realize that although it's important, marriage has really nothing to do with sex; it's about genuine love; clear-headed love and so much more which is what promotes longevity. It now occurs to me, that it is a simple business contract that must start with a "flame" but grows to be a willing commitment to "stick by" that special person.

Two people must have a certain level of refinement to maintain a marriage. This is why you don't necessarily have to dress sexy to "get a man" because that's not what shines through to a man who's looking for a wife. This is why the amount of education or material possessions do not necessarily matter either. There is a great passage in the book *It can Happen to You: The Practical Guide to Romantic Love* by Dr. Roger Callahan and Karen Levine, which depicts an introduction of a newly married couple to their wedding guests and practically and perfectly explains the union of marriage. Part of it is recorded below:

The ceremony which we are about to perform will not unite you in marriage. Only you can do that. The union that you are about to publicly formalize is not a casual one and not to be taken lightly, but the most important into which you will ever enter. If the relationship between two people, which is symbolized in our culture by the state of marriage, does not already exist between you, this ceremony will not create it. This ceremony is simply the public announcement of the existence of that relationship. The state, the church, or any other agency can only give its recognition to the bond between you. The state of marriage can exist between two people only when they wish it to exist and it does at that my moment come to be. As you give public announcement to the existence of the bond uniting you by means of this ceremony which you are about to perform, keep in mind that you, together, have created this marriage.

The passages in the introduction explain that each person in the marriage is their own individual and each should have mutual respect for the other as individuals and for their achievements. To me this means that in order to have a healthy marriage both parties must already be whole and there is also a certain level of refinement that must exist, individually.

I also like what Marilyn Hickey shared in her sermon on *Breaking Generational Curses*. She suggests that one key to a man's desire to marry you is to let him "cover" you; meaning, there has to be a sincere desire in you to want him to protect you. Also, though I understand that some of these ideas may be antiquated, in Mary C. Crowley's book, *You Can Too*, she suggests that a woman should make sure the home is clean and peaceful so that he will want to come home to it. We live in such an egalitarian society these days so these ideas may or may not work for some. Not all marriages or relationships are created equal, so to speak. I, however do agree with the ideas suggested above. I also agree that the union is a partnership and each member should work to enhance the other's life. I believe that each person's job in the relationship is to help make the other's life a little easier.

Chapter 17

Recurring Themes

I have often heard many of the greats posit how important it is to recognize themes and/or patterns in one's life. Allender (2005) states that we must be curious and open so that we may learn who we are. I also read somewhere that society will tell you who you are. Allender goes on to state that throughout our lifetime others have named us; some good and some bad. However, it is up to us to connect the dots. This is how we grow. "Listen to your life." he states. "It will give you countless words that describe your way of being, relating and engaging others." He urges us to listen to our stories as they will reveal a pattern of roles we've played. He goes on to state, however, that we should rightly read those themes and/or patterns. A life theme, he asserts, sets the trajectory of or lives and that trajectory is often woven into the role that we are to play.

I know I've always loved people. I love meeting interesting, level-headed, intelligent, fun, and funny people who are nice and who like to contribute to the well-being of others. No matter where I find myself, I always find a church to join; a place I can get involved in on a community level. I always find myself as a member of a gym and some sort of performing arts class. All this to say that I love interacting with people. That is my nature.

Prior to my career in clinical research thirteen years ago, the only work I did was in the helping profession. Right out of college I worked as an education coordinator for an after-school program for at-risk youth. After that I worked as a therapeutic support staff (TSS) for the same population. Subsequently I worked as a worksite placement specialist for welfare recipients. Ever since my junior year in high school, I knew I wanted to be a psychologist. I've always been interested in human behavior, though I left the human services field when I was 30 for financial reasons. While working in clinical research, I was able to make a very good living for my son and me. However, I eventually felt out of place which is why I got out of that field. I needed to help people on a more micro level. I always return to serving humanity in some way.

I have noticed several themes throughout my life, both positive and negative. One negative theme that keeps coming up in my life is that of isolation. Ironic since I love being around people, right? I know it's not my true personality to be isolated. I recall that as a teenager, while living at my grandmother's, I was not allowed to talk on the phone with my peers. Back then, before the prevalence of cell phones, it was possible to set your landline to have separate rings for different numbers. For example, the phone sounded two rings when someone was calling for my brother and there was just one ring when someone was calling the main house phone number. I was just a non-factor and not allowed to receive phone calls or talk on the phone at all. I knew back then that this would affect my life as an adult. In addition, I don't have the same two parents as the rest of my siblings so I was never fully able to compare myself, my personality, and development with anyone. I felt no one could really relate to me. Although I had friends growing up, no one could understand the issues I had with my grandmother. People thought I was crazy when I told them of the abuse I was enduring at her hands. I'm now a grandmother myself and I know Johnathan would not be able to relate to anyone talking about their grandmother the way I did. He is adored and loved by me and waited on hand and foot.

Additionally, for a long time I never really felt "Black" enough. Coming from McKinley to Abington I didn't feel like I completely fit in with the Black kids because while McKinley in those days was only about 3% Black and about 95% White. Because I wasn't raised in the church, I did not get that Black cultural experience nor did I come home to a Black family rich in Black culture, therefore, my Black identity was lost. It ended up being easier for me to relate to the ambiguous identity of those who were half Black and half White, perhaps because they also felt that they never quite fit in.

While I went to North Philly on the weekends and during the summer months, I only associated with close family and friends and it wasn't for any prolonged period of time. In those days in Abington Township at least, it seemed most of the families were pretty much intact. And most people had one or two parents that cared about them, at least enough to have the proper school supplies. I will say however that when I was with my dad, proper school supplies were a priority. He also made sure I had other things that helped me fit into society, but it remained that while we appeared middle-class, the spirit in the home and with which I was raised was impoverished.

When I went to Cheyney, an HBCU, I didn't have a microwave, TV, or a refrigerator filled with food like the others did so I didn't feel like I fit in with the students there either. Ironically, I didn't fit in with the students who were born and raised in the inner city because I had attended a suburban school. There were just many times when I felt alone.

Because of the township in which I was raised, I didn't live up to the stereotypical traits of being "loud" and "bold" with a "strong" personality that we frequently see reflected in the media; nor were pride or respect instilled in me, so again there was that constant theme of not quite belonging anywhere.

Thankfully over time, I've come to realize that I belong exactly where I am. I know I've worked really hard to accomplish much in my life and I feel that I should be accepted for that. Not because I'm this great person but because I am me---flaws and all. We are all human and imperfect, however, I am also educated and therefore feel I can relate to and understand most anyone. The book *Winning in the Land of Giants* is about people seeing you as you see yourself. Many people try to hide how they truly feel about themselves, thinking they are fooling others. They are only fooling themselves. People know the truth even if they don't have the words or theories to explain how they are feeling. For example, if you see yourself as an ant people will see you as such. The same is true if you see yourself as a giant. If you see yourself as belonging and accepting of others, people will generally see you that same way. If you see yourself as confident and worthy of respect; people will see you that way as well.

Allender believes that a life theme sets the trajectory of our lives and that trajectory is woven into the roles we are to play. He also says that as we read and reread our story, we will notice some patterns and with time, prayer, and reflection, we will eventually see the contours of our path come into focus. I am praying this is true.

One theme I've recognized is that I feel nobody wants me so I have this looming energy that reflects that fact: that I am unwanted. When I disclosed this to my therapist, she suggested I ask people who know me and whom I respect what they think of me. I have asked a few people, many of which never gave me feedback, probably because they're afraid they're going to hurt my feelings. Others told me that I'm just too hard on myself. The family in which I was raised was always judgmental towards me. Because of this, I believe that most of my life I have unconsciously chosen to interact with mostly judgmental people. It's familiar territory to me.

The biggest theme in my life, however, remains isolation. Sometimes, it even seems like there's an unseen force constantly pushing me out to the margins of society. It has to do with the core beliefs I have about myself which started in childhood. In Wallace D. Wattles book, *The Science of Getting Rich*, he states that combatting this is the "hardest work in the world." I also read somewhere that this is why one should not try to change anyone. If you know how hard it is to change your own core beliefs, you should come to the realization that it's impossible to change anyone else's. I think the best way to remedy our struggle with rejection and isolation is to love and accept ourselves as we are. It's truly an inside job.

Chapter 18

Success Principles (some)

Throughout my life, I have realized some things worked for me in accomplishing my goals and maintaining resiliency. Conversely, there are some things I noticed I was lacking whereas I saw those same things in other people which caused them to be successful. I strive to incorporate all of life's success principles to become the best person I can be. Below, I list some of these principles and elaborate on these success principles.

Movement

Why is Movement so important? Well, "movement is life, and we're always in motion, even while asleep" (Travis and Ryan, 2004). The most enticing and rewarding benefit of movement is that exercise increases endorphin levels (the feel-good hormones) in the blood stream. Exercise is key in treating physical and mental health concerns like depression, anxiety, backaches, diabetes, arthritis, and so much more. In the world of fitness, wellness, and mental health therapy, it is a known fact that simply moving is a frequently prescribed antidote. The assertion, "the more you move, the better you feel" is true. Also, we must remember to stretch! I have found that stretching releases many negative emotions. I always feel better after I stretch. I use the same stretch routine I learned in gymnastics when I was 14 years old. But you can Google to find one that works best for you.

Many spiritual practices speak of the mind, body, and soul connection. I have found this to be true as well. There was a time in my life when I would go to Zumba (dance class) two or three times a week then go swimming that Saturday after Zumba. I felt like I looked my best. I walked with my head held high and with so much confidence. My thinking was clear and just being in the water positively affected my mood and spiritual life. I was just happier and more easily gave thanks.

Arloski (2014) speaks of a similar experience when he began a workout routine in his mid-50's. He stated that he began working out six days a week, including strength training and that he also began a healthy eating regimen. He says that he felt great and that his energy level was more constant throughout the day. I can attest to this. It's as if the more consistent and comprehensive your daily physical exercise routine is, the more positively it affects every aspect of your life. It is as if it becomes part of who you are and everyone can see it. But even more, you feel it!

1 Corinthians 6:19-20 states that your body is the temple of the Holy Spirit and 1 Corinthians 3:16 states that God's spirit dwells within you. If the Holy

Spirit is the Holy Spirit of God dwelling in you, it would only make sense that we take care of our temple by building it up to its potential, complementing our enhancement of mental, spiritual, and emotional health. Perhaps, the Holy Spirit is what shines through when we treat our body the way it should be treated.

Finally, Travis and Ryan (2004) assert that some of the signs that indicate it's time to start moving include tense muscles, restricted range of motion, shallow breathing, and overall fatigue. He said we should practice noticing when those muscles need to be moved.

Respectability

According to Huo and Binning (2008), respect can take on the form of attitudes as varied as regard for social rules and the sharing of power in groups. It can also be defined as respect for another group member or leader, affective evaluation, and status evaluation. My lack of respect came from my first point of reference; my family. I was simply not seen; especially in a positive light. Several online sources define respect as:

1. The state or quality of being proper, correct, and socially acceptable.
2. The state or quality of being accepted as valid or important within a particular field.
3. A feeling of appreciative, often courteous regard; esteem

Huo and Binning posit that the two motives for which people aim for respect are: the status motive and the belongingness motive. They assert that having a high status within a group can predict social power, psychological well-being, and good physical health. While respect pertains to the belongingness motive, Huo and Binning state that people desire respect because of the simple human need to feel they belong. One study found that respectful treatment increases individuals' perception that they are welcome or accepted within a group in which they are a member.

It stands to reason that one who is not embraced or accepted by their family, their first point of reference, might find it difficult to be accepted or embraced outside of their family. Because a person doesn't feel that they can command respect, they end up feeling disrespected because of their most prominent experience (in this case family). I would like to add that you can command respect but you cannot demand respect. It doesn't work that way. Everything comes from within. How might you command respect if you've never felt respected? The following outlines some of the ways to do so:

1. Put God first in everything you do
2. Start by respecting others
3. Carry yourself with dignity
4. Don't tolerate anything less than respect from others
5. Be trustworthy

6. Be true to your word
7. Take pride in everything you do
8. Never rest on your laurels (Crowley, 2000)
9. Expect respect...because you are doing your best

When people feel respected, they function better and have better efficacy. And those who are not respected demonstrate feelings of shame (Huo & Benning, 2008). Shame is defined as a painful emotion caused by the belief that one is, or is perceived by others to be, inferior or unworthy of affection or respect because of one's actions, thoughts, circumstances, or experiences. Sometimes we believe the lie that we are not worthy of respect. But everyone is worthy of respect. Richard Sennett (2003) states that "unlike food, respect costs nothing..." Therefore, we should not accept anything less.

Value

Jim Rohn says that to add value to yourself invest in yourself. I would add that if you want to be valuable, contribute a great deal to the groups to which you belong. In the movie *The Secret* they talk about the importance of filling yourself up so that you have an abundant amount to *give; as the Bible says, "pressed down, shaken together, running over" (Luke 6:38, KJV).*

Confidence

Confidence is key. It is everything. Confidence is the *thing* that literally pulls things toward us; people, opportunities, etc. From my experience, we gain confidence by accomplishing things we set out to do. Confidence also comes from believing in yourself. It doesn't matter what anyone else thinks about you. People have their own issues. It only matters what you think about yourself and what you can do. How can you build confidence? Challenge yourself to learn new skills, try new things. Any area in which you don't feel confident, get coaching, enroll in a class, engage in self-improvement.

Self-Esteem

Healthy self-esteem comes from being aware of our positive qualities and characteristics. The more positive accomplishments and capabilities, the higher a person's self-esteem will be. On the other hand, low self-esteem is commonly associated with feelings of worthlessness and depression. It stands to reason that boosting one's self-esteem is accomplished by increasing positive accomplishments and boosting positive characteristics. You've got to get involved in new things, and push yourself to finish what you start. Learn a new skill, develop a talent, learn to dance and anything else that makes you feel good about yourself. There's a misconception that self-esteem comes from looking good and having nice things. Though that may help a little, it's only fleeting. True self-esteem is realizing your fundamental worth.

Power

There are so many Biblical scriptures pertaining to power. We have power. We have the power to create the life we want. We do. One of my favorite scriptures is "To whom God would make known what is the riches of the glory of this mystery amount the Gentiles, which is Christ in you, the hope of glory" (Col 1:27, *KJV*). And 1 Corinthians 1:24 (*KJV*) states, "but unto them which are called, both Jews and Greeks, Christ the power of God and the wisdom of God." We have this power living on the inside of us. In fact, the scripture states that God frowns upon those that appear to be "Christians" but do not use the power that God has given to them. In 2 Timothy 3:5 (*KJV*), it is stated, "Having a form of godliness, but denying the power thereof: from such turn away."

Self-image

This is the way we see ourselves. It usually stems from how our primary caregivers saw us or what they projected onto us as we were being raised. The result can be empowering or damaging, depending on who our caregivers were. John Mawell Maltz, author of *The New Psychocybernetics*, says that we cannot do anything that deviates from this image that we have of ourselves. But we must internalize and know that we are made in the image and likeness of God. We must learn to see ourselves as God sees us. Finally, envision who you know you are inside and go out into the world as that person.

Eating

The medical community is realizing more and more that food can be used for medicinal purposes. For example, I used to have major issues with constipation. Instead of using over-the-counter laxatives, I asked my doctor what natural remedies I could use. She recommended oranges! They are rich in fiber and when eaten along with drinking a good amount of water, it works for me every time.

We all know how important water is. Our bodies are 70% water and our brains are 75% water. That alone tells us how important it is that we consume the proper amount of water. According to Travis and Ryan (2004), the exact amount of water we should drink daily depends on many factors (i.e., temperature in the air, your physical activity, etc.). Typically, it is recommended to drink at least 64 ounces of water a day (Travis & Ryan, 2004), however, just like with any other healthcare regimen, always consult a medical professional prior to initiation to determine what is best for you.

Additionally, we need plenty of protein. Our bodies are comprised chiefly of proteins (Travis & Ryan, 2004), so it stands to reason that we must eat a sufficient amount to replenish what is lost daily. And it doesn't have to be in the form of meat. We can eat nuts, legumes, soybeans, and even some fruits and vegetables contain protein (avocado, guava, spinach, brussel sprouts, etc.). Finally, we should be eating plenty of thoroughly cleaned raw vegetables and fruits. If you feel you won't eat all of your fresh produce before they expire then frozen fruits and vegetables are a good substitute (Travis & Ryan, 2004). Eating fresh, healthy foods and drinking plenty of water can make a world of difference in terms of how we feel and function. One should never underestimate a good food diet along the road to self-actualization and beyond.

We are all works in progress but if we wish to become successful, we have to save ourselves. You can start slowly if necessary, by gradually employing the above-named practices into your life one at a time and work on making them part of your lifestyle. Start by committing to 21 days which is the time it takes to create new habits.

It's okay if we occasionally "fall off" as we learn. We have to give ourselves permission to be human. Just get back on track as soon as you can. As long as we're actively trying no one can fault us, not even ourselves. We are doing our best. Finally, I believe that words are powerful, so when we find ourselves struggling in an area, it helps to read peer-reviewed articles, books, or even watch videos on a subject, then boldly put what we've learned into to practice.

Chapter 19

My Passion

What moves you most deeply? What do you most enjoy doing? Where do you find the greatest pleasure and joy? What is it about this activity, idea or person that makes you feel alive? This is easy for me to answer; believe it or not, I still love to perform, sing and dance. Allender (2005) speaks of the ideal self. This is the way we see ourselves in terms of values, beliefs and dreams. The ought self is what others expect us to be and the real self is the person who lives in the middle, between the ideal self and the ought self.

My ideal self would have been a stage performer on Broadway; my practical self, a therapist. As previously mentioned, while growing up I loved musicals. Unfortunately, my mother frequently told me I couldn't possibly make a living performing in musicals and that I needed to "get in the real world." But that *was* my "real" world. In elementary school and junior high school, I felt most alive when I was performing in some way. My dad was supportive. He enrolled me in acting classes and set up interviews with casting directors. There are many performing artists on my dad's side, so he understood my love of the arts.

On my mom's side however, they were all working to middle class "workers;" educated, but workers. I was heartbroken when my mom recently disclosed to me, that she too had aspirations of becoming a dancer and that she was cast to dance in the movie *Cleopatra*. She was so excited when she landed the part, but her father told her that she couldn't perform in the movie and to "get in the real world." She told me that it took a long time before she got up the courage to watch the movie. When I discovered that she'd kept this story to herself all this time, and had been told to "get in the real world" just like she'd done me, I felt betrayed and played. I'd literally come by my talents honestly and she never let on to this. This could have united us in a common passion for the performing arts, but instead she just shut my dream down. The thought that someone could completely withhold that fact from their child for 40 years was disturbing to me to say the least. I thought, "she literally has attempted to destroy every aspect of my life." I came to realize that I had to have limited contact with her, because she constantly tries to shut my goals and dreams down, then laughs at me when she feels I haven't "measured up" to my peers...

John 10:10 states: "the enemy comes to kill, steal, and destroy." It stands to reason that if God placed a desire within you and someone attempts to extinguish that desire, they are certainly not working with God to help you realize your destiny. And to this point, I think about a quote from Terence, "I am a man, I consider nothing that is human alien to me." We are human, anything that any other human can do is possible for us to do as well, be it good or bad.

My ideal self, however, is not lost. I love counseling, learning about human behavior, and helping others. In fact, ideally my life would consist of both counseling and performing in musicals. I can still do this. Though I may seem reserved, I come alive on stage. When I'm dancing, I get so caught up that I dance like nobody's watching. I feel like a leader, like I own it. I feel the same way with counseling. My mom tried to talk me out of my love for counselling too, saying, "you're disturbed; how are you going to help anyone else." Sadly, from my relationships, to my vocation, to my social life...most times where I've experienced a loss of some kind, my mom's voice is echoing in the background. I'm not blaming her solely nor am I mad with her. Also, I'm not trying to play the victim...this is just my experience.

We have to forgive so that we may be forgiven. Many wonder how you can tell if you've truly forgiven someone. So far Charles Stanley has the best definition: "You know you have forgiven them when you don't hold it against them anymore." Sadly, many people tend to inflict the very thing that was done to them on others. Hurting people, hurt people. Healed people, heal people.

Because of everything I've been through and learned, I know I am a great asset to others, teaching and helping to guide them in the right direction. This helps me to feel that I'm walking in my purpose. It makes me feel alive. I'm so happy that the Christ that lives in me did not waiver. He was going to have his way in my life no matter what. And he has. I love Philippians 2:12: "Work out your salvation with fear and trembling," and Philippians 2:13: "For it is God which worketh in you both to will and to do of his good pleasure" (*KJV*). At some point, we have to move forward and live the life our creator planned for us.

I believe that everyone has a purpose for their life. It starts when you are a little kid. If you can just get on the "God wave," as I like to call it, or stay on the "correct" ladder, your life won't be in vain. All of the obstacles don't matter. If you're still here, there is still work to be done. How do you get on the God wave you may ask? If you've been through tons of obstacles doesn't it throw you off? Everything that happens in life is definitely preparing you for what you are supposed to do. You just have to pay attention. How do you pay attention? Your hard times are a reminder to you that allow you to help others who may be going through those same hard times. If you can at least touch one person, maybe that person won't have to go through what you went through. If you are inclined to do the hard work to recover and be restored, and when the opportunity presents itself you share your story: that is your part in making this world a better place.

In one of the textbooks used in my counseling program, I learned about organismic value processing, which is a concept brought forth by Carl Rogers. Essentially, healthy individuals have such healthy self-esteem, that they do not just accept whomever comes along in their lives. Instead, they determine whether or not that individual is going to make them a better person then decide intentionally whether or not they want that person in their life. We cannot select our family of course, but when I heard of this concept, I started being much more selective of not only the people I wanted in my life but also the events I chose to participate in.

Being selective in relationships is a good way people can avoid drama in their lives. However, we must be aware of such and have the courage to stand alone at times when the right person for the mission is not present. Sometimes I've felt the need to take whomever comes along and just be happy that someone is interested in me whether it's a friendship or a romance. One thing for sure, we all want to be happy, but we can't truly be happy if we're not true to ourselves first. Being alone is not my first choice but I'm definitely not afraid to stand alone.

Allender (2005) wrote that God has written a story for my life, so I guess I have to learn to somehow be okay with everything that has occurred. I sometimes question why God would write such a story? Why would He write a story for a young lady who had to work so hard and sacrifice the very social life that she considered the dominant growth factor of her life? Why would He let an innocent baby grow up without a positive male role-model and live in an incredibly dysfunctional family? Perhaps it was God's will so that I would simply grow closer to Him. I was not raised to go to church regularly, but after my son was born, we became regular church-goers. I got closer to God than I could ever have imagined and in my opinion, learned to be more Christ-like than almost anyone in my family. At the time my son was conceived, I had been veering off track socially and it probably would eventually have killed me, at least spiritually.

I pray that God continues His will for me, my son's and now my grandson's, and allows His greatest story about Himself to be revealed through us. Allender also states that we should be living our life most consistent with how He has been writing our life story. In high school, although I loved my psychology class, I really wanted to be a news anchor. Though I completed broadcasting school, as I matured, I realized that I love the on-air component of radio and I like more behind the scenes TV production unless it's a show where the focus is on a discussion, not news reporting. I also realized that I could be more effective by focusing on laws and principles, and by helping people live the life God desires for them. I also learned many Biblical principles in grad school. Perhaps this was His plan all along and had I not had my son when I did, I would not have taken the same path, that of seeking to help so many others along this journey called life.

I love when Allender says that God is waiting to be revealed in our story and all we have to do is ask, seek, and knock. He also states that the purpose of tragedy is to wake us up to move us in His direction for our lives. Was that second "ladder" God's will all along?

Chapter 20

Hope and a Future

According to Orbeke and Smith (2012), resiliency is a phenomenon that includes two factors; (1) exposure to adverse or traumatic conditions and (2) successful adaptation following that exposure. Hence, one cannot be considered resilient if there isn't some significant stressor to overcome. So, what is "successful adaption?" It seems to me it means that you've experienced specific trauma or traumas and recognized them and in the long run they haven't interfered with your personality, vocation, or relationships.

In *The Strangest Secret*, Earl Nightingale defines success as, "the progressive realization of a worthy ideal or goal." I think the operative word there is "progressive." Obstacles will come but we must keep going; keep progressing toward our goal. I'm still a work in progress and always will be.

According to Yehuda, Flory, Southwick, and Charney (2006), resiliency is defined as the process of adapting well in the face of adversity. According to Bogar and Hulse (2006), resiliency is conceptualized as a combination of organic personality traits and environmental influence that serve as protection from harmful psychological effects of trauma and severe stress, enabling the individual to lead a satisfying and productive life. Another term used to describe resiliency is hardiness. Those who are not significantly or negatively affected by stress can be characterized as hardy (Feldman, 2014).

In his research, Adams (1973) asks several questions in terms of extreme abuse by one's parents. He sought to discover whether it put a child at risk for a disadvantaged life or not. I'm not saying that I was extremely abused however, throughout my life and in my work, I've witnessed the damage that can emanate following such treatment. Adams posits that such harm would inevitably cause one to "deviate from normal living patterns," so much so that the child becomes abnormal. He responds that the effects of physical abuse can appear later on in life and that the effects may be lasting. While this may be true for some, other survivors of abuse show outstanding resiliency.

Having expressed this, I cannot stress enough that when your kids are at the age of making choices about what they like to do or have an interest in, allow them to make their own decisions and trust that you instilled proper values in them. Otherwise, it will throw them completely off course. Do not take their agency away or squash their dreams as it can take away their power and efficacy. My parents didn't really know me, at least not in the same way I knew my son, especially throughout his formative years.

My parents and I never lived together for any significant period of time nor did we have the same mailing address. Whereas, I knew everything about my son and I took pride in that. No one could tell me anything about him that I didn't already know. It's important to let your children use their agency and direct their own lives, especially if you don't know what they're capable of. We don't always know what they are capable of but they do. A capable, competent person must use their agency to direct their lives.

My son was so beautiful and perfect when they rolled him into my room, that I may have decided on my own to keep him with me instead of wanting to give him up for adoption. But it would have been my decision either way. It's important not to take a person's agency or power away from them, particularly when it involves life-altering decisions. Doing so could cause much conflict and confusion in their lives. It can throw their whole life off balance, having them try to live a life they had not envisioned for themself, thus taking away their identity. They can begin to feel like a misfit.

I simply wasn't nurtured or properly prepared for life, I worked hard to be an upstanding person. Attending a good school district and having my dad in my life helped, but I basically raised myself. Besides my dad's expectations for me, nothing was ever really expected of me. I realize now that for much of my life I was sad and unfulfilled. I didn't grow up among the conventional lines of development that carry over into other aspects of daily living.

When I think of the question, "well, Karima, what events from your past are easy to see as God's will? Which events are struggles to accept as God's will?" I think about many things. Certain things that can happen in a person's life have the tendency to take their power away. We all need to be empowered. 2 Timothy 3:5 speaks of people "having a form of godliness, but denying the power thereof." This scripture goes on to state that we should stay away from such people. What this means to me is that people that are about something should stay away from people who lack confidence in themselves and even more so, in the power that God gave each one of us to affect our lives for the positive.

As a young person raising a child by myself, my family took so much of my power away. That could have also contributed to some of the isolation I experienced. God wanted my son to be born. People have miscarriages all the time. I did not, so God wanted my son to be here. His earthly parents were the vessel God used to get him here. I see God's will being done in his life. Matthew excels at everything he chooses to do. He writes something down then sees it come to fruition. He has power and uses it when he wants to.

He is beautiful and smart. While he was growing up, I instilled in him that he deserves to be respected and that he should always speak up for himself. He's currently, a lyricist and has a golden voice. He's been performing on stage since he was in elementary school; then professionally during his high school years, early adulthood, and to this day. My son struggles with his self-image at times however as evidenced by the hurt expressed in his lyrics and sometimes when he addresses me. He has no problems advocating for himself though.

Though there were times when I wondered if it was in fact God's will for my son to be raised by me in my family with no real moral or social support, I have come to realize that it was God's plan all along. Though he and I struggled through some hard times, and though my mind had me wondering if maybe God had in fact wanted me to give him up for adoption, the fact that he was handed to me to raise is confirmation that he is in exactly the right place. Yes, he may have had it easier if placed in a two-parent family with two healthy parents (male and female) who could raise him in a Godly and healthy home environment, but he would've always longed to get to know me and would've potentially had some of the same challenges. I really believe that part of my desire to give him up for adoption was because I didn't want him to grow up in my dysfunctional family.

I genuinely love my son and I am grateful for him. God is not finished with Matthew yet, nor do we know what He has in store for Johnathan...Either way, I know He has a plan.

Allender (2005) says that we want to be freed from our problems so we can get on with our pleasures. But God wants our problems to serve as a context for knowing Him and living out the story He writes for His glory. He states that the present is not meant merely to be resolved, or even learned from, but to be written in a way that allows us to reveal God to others and to ourselves. If this is the case, it makes it all worth it. I've learned not to question God. "For my thoughts are not your thoughts, neither are your ways my ways, saith the Lord" (Johnathan 55:8, *KJV*). "God causes all things to work together for good for those who love God, to them who are called according to His purpose" (Romans 8:28, *KJV*).

People come into the world under all types of circumstances and yet still find a way to thrive. My pastor in Tampa often shared that he came into the world as a result of rape. Although my son didn't come into this world under the most ideal circumstances, and I wasn't ready for a child, I am comforted by the fact that I did right by him, raising him the best I could. I think of Matthew 21:28-31: "A certain man had two sons; and he came to the first, and said, son, go work today in my vineyard. He answered and said, I will not: but afterward he repented, and went. And he came to the second, and said likewise. And he answered and said, I go, sir: and went not. Whether of them twain did the will of his father? They say unto him, the first" (*KJV*).

There is something redeeming about telling my story; vindicating, even. If you're so led, I urge you to write your story too. Do not die with your story still inside you. It could help many others and it is very empowering particularly if you felt that your power was taken away from you like mine was. It doesn't happen overnight but when you write your story, "it's all out there." No one can hold anything against you or throw it back in your face. I love what Michelle Obama wrote: "if you don't get out there and define yourself, you'll be quickly and inaccurately defined by others. James Baldwin said, "you have to impose, in fact – this may sound very strange – you have to decide who you are, and force the world to deal with you; not with its idea of you." It's so true. You have to live out loud. Not only will society try to tell you who you are; I've found that people will distort who you are. They want to project their idea of you onto you. Sometimes it's good and sometimes it's bad. I urge you to tell your own story...Live out loud.

If you want to know what your true calling is, simply look no further than to what you gravitate towards every day. If people seek you out for certain things then that is what you're meant to be doing. So far, God has allowed some of my dreams to come true. I may seem like a late bloomer, but it's all about His timing, not mine. After all, I spent nearly 20 years of my adult life raising a child. I put a lot of my dreams on hold, but they are still in me, moving me forward towards the day that I materialize them. I know that there are a lot of great things in store for me. "For I know the thoughts that I think toward you, saith the Lord, thoughts of peace and not of evil, to give you an expected end" (Jeremiah 29.11, *KJV*). Some versions read, "He will give you hope and a future." God will give you beauty for your ashes. I believe it's in *The Alchemist* by Paulo Coelho that he writes of how we can turn the lead in our lives to gold. Finally, I think of Mark 11:23 "Truly, I say unto you, whoever says to this mountain, 'Be taken up and thrown into the sea,' and does not doubt in his heart, but believes that what he says will come to pass, it will be done for him." What are your "mountains?" Tell them to move and believe in your heart that they will indeed be moved and watch God work...

Yes, I have been through a lot. It is not always easy but as I mentioned in "About the Cover", it is life – many mountains and valleys. Joel Osteen said that whenever you've gone through something you become uniquely qualified to help somebody else. Whatever the enemy meant for harm; God will turn around for our good. So, learn to consider your trials as blessings. That's what I hope to do with my book and my work. I lived and grew through everything I've gone through because God trusted in me that I would bless others and teach others. So, I've learned to embrace everything that has happened to me and most of all, I am thankful for my beautiful son and grandson. I am blessed that they are in my life.

God entrusted me with them and kept me through all of my trials. He blessed me with a father who inspired me and motivated me to spread my wings. And a mother whom I love dearly. He gave me a brother and a sister, whom I love, he allowed me to go to good schools and to experience all sorts of interesting things. He gave me a good mind and a strong drive to succeed. And now I am a published author! In spite of all my trials, He knew that one day I would be in a position to encourage and help others because of my story. It's been part of His plan all along...He truly has given me hope and a future.

References

1. APA College Dictionary of Psychology (2009). Washington, DC. (372-373)

2. Adams, J. E. (1973). The Christian Counselor's Manual. Grand Rapids, MI: Zondervan Publishing House.

3. Adler, L. & Riss, S. (Producer), & Sendak, M. (Director). (1975). *Really Rosie* [Motion Picture]. USA: Children's Circle.

4. Allender, D. (2005). *To be Told.* Colorado Springs, CO. Waterbrook.

5. Angelou, M. [Maya Angelou]. (2020, January 24). Maya Angelou Interview [Video]. YouTube. https://youtu.be/q6WqYMdRIRI

6. Arloski, M. (2014). *Wellness coaching for lasting lifestyle change 2nd Ed.* Duluth, MN. Whole Person

7. American Psychiatric Association. (2013). *Diagnostic and statistical manual of mental disorders* (5th ed.). Washington, DC: Author.

8. Bogar, C. B. & Hulse, D. (2006). Resiliency determinants and resiliency processes among female adult survivors of childhood sexual abuse. *Journal of Counseling & Development*, 84, 318-327

9. Burton, Valorie. (2012). *Successful women think differently.* Eugene, Oregon. Harvest House.

10. Covey, S. R. (2004). The *7 habits of highly effective people*: Restoring the character ethic. New York: Free Press. Goldenberg, H., & Goldenberg, I. (2013). *Family therapy: An overview* (8th ed.). Belmont, CA: Brooks/Cole Publishing Co.

11. Coelho, P. (1998). *The alchemist.* San Francisco: Harper San Francisco.

12. Crowley, M. (2000). *You can too.* Revell. Ada, MI.

13. Doweiko, H. (2015). *Concepts of chemical dependency, 9th Edition.* Cengage Learning. Stamford, Ct.

14. Feldman, R. S. (2014). *Development across the life span* (Custom 7th ed.). Boston, MA: Pearson.

15. Goulston, M. & Goldberg, P. (1996). *Get out of your own way.* New York, NY. Berkley.

16. Haanel, C. (Unknown). *The master key system.* USA. Costa Books.

17. Hickey, M. (2013). *Breaking generational curses.* https://youtu.be/ Hj8NokGteg . YouTube.

18. Hill, Napoleon. (2003). *Think and grow rich.* New York, NY. Penguin.

19. Huo, Y. & Binning, K. (2008). *Why the Psychological Experience of Respect Matters in Group Life: An Integrative Account.* Social and Personality Psychology Compass 2 10.1111/j.1751-9004.2008.00129.x

20. Hulst, D. (Unknown). *As a woman thinketh.* Camarillo, CA: DeVorss.

21. Klika, J. B. & Herrenkohl, T.I. (2013). A review of developmental research on resilience in maltreated children. *Trauma, Violence & Abuse*, 14*(3)*, 222-234. doi: 10.1177/1524838013487808

22. Maltz, M. (2002). *The new psycho-cybernetics.* Saddle River, NJ. Prentice Hall Press.

23. Maslov's Hierarchy of Needs. https://www.gettingsmart.com/2019/10/4-holistic-classroom-ideas-inspired-by-maslows-humanist-approach/

24. McBride, K. (2008). *Will I ever be good enough.* New York, NY. Atria.

25. McGraw, P. (2012). *Life code.* Los Angeles, CA. Bird Street Books.

26. Mitchell, W. (1995). *Winning in the land of giants.* Nashville, TN. Thomas Nelson, Inc.

27. Nightingale, E. (2013). *Audiobook – The Strangest Secret* by Earl Nightingale. https://youtu.be/mU_PExRRb38. YouTube.

28. Obama, M. (2018). *Becoming.* New York, NY. *Crown Publishing Group.*

29. Orbke, S., & Smith, H.L. (2013). *A* developmental framework for enhancing resiliency in adult survivors

of childhood abuse. *International Journal for the Advancement of Counselling. 35(1)*, 46-56. doi: 10.1007/s10447-012-9164-6

30. Sennett, R. (2003). *Respect in a World of In Equality.* New York, NY. W. W. Norton & Company, Inc.

31. Smith, R. (2006). *Lies at the altar: The truth about great marriages.* New York, NY. Hyperion.

32. Spurgeon, C. (2009). *The prayer of Jabez.* Kindle Edition. Habakkuk Books.

33. Travis, J. & Ryan, S. (2004). *Wellness workbook: How to Achieve Enduring Health and Vitality.* Ten Speed Press. New York, NY.

34. Trudeau, K. [Kevin Trudeau]. (2017, January 4). Your Wish is Your Command [Video]. YouTube. https://youtu.be/DZz2eK9zAFQ

35. Twerski, A. (1991). Let us make man: Self-esteem through Jewishness. C.I.S. Publishers and Distributors. Lakewood, NJ.

36. Wattles, W. (1910). *The science of getting rich.* Holyoke, MA. Elizabeth Towne.

37. Yehuda, R., Flory, J. D., Southwick, S., Charney, D. S. (2006). Developing an agenda for translational studies of resilience and vulnerability following trauma exposure. *Annals New York Academy of Sciences,* 1071, 379-396. doi: 10.1196/annals.1364.028

38. Callahan, R. and Levine, K. (1982). It can happen to you: The practical guide to romantic love. A & W Publishers, Inc. New York, NY.

Printed in Great Britain
by Amazon

82015175R00132